NULLITY OF MARRIAGE

NULLITY
of
MARRIAGE

New Edition—Revised and Enlarged

F. J. Sheed

SHEED AND WARD · NEW YORK

Library of Congress Catalog Card Number 59-10656

NIHIL OBSTAT:

JOHN R. READY

CENSOR LIBRORUM

MAY 22, 1959

IMPRIMATUR:

✠ ROBERT F. JOYCE

BISHOP OF BURLINGTON

MAY 28, 1959

MANUFACTURED IN THE UNITED STATES OF AMERICA

TO THE LAW SCHOOL
OF THE UNIVERSITY OF SYDNEY
THIS SMALL TOKEN
OF GREAT GRATITUDE

Preface to the Second Edition

This is not a book on marriage; but only on those cases where marriage appears to be but is not. It is directly concerned with the law of the Catholic Church, but in the first edition I introduced comparisons with the law of England. I have been asked to introduce comparisons with American Law as well, because its historic connection with Church Law is considerably less than England's. As each of the fifty States has its own marriage law, and it would have been impossible to study them all, I chose that of New York. New York's Marriage Law was not taught in the Sydney University Law School in my day, as any American who chances on this book will guess. But its rules, like those of England, are stated here only in their general form, exceptions or modifications not being mentioned where they would not affect the principle. The subject of the book is Church Law.

The object of the comparison is not to make civil law and Church law look as much alike as possible, in the hope that the great mass of similarity may lead to an indulgent overlooking of the points on which the Church differs; but to show her laws more clearly by noting how two other codes treat the same problems. The book's purpose is to show the Church's law of Nullity as it is—a strong and clearly-defined system, wonderfully reasoned and consistent with itself. I do not wish to defend it or prove its rightness, but only to *state* it; and this not so much for its own sake as for the light it sheds on the nature of marriage.

The value of the similarities to be found in the English law of Nullity lies in the differences which four hundred years of separation have produced in other parts of the marriage law. Where two authorities so different in outlook and method apply the same law to a given subject as England and Rome do to Nullity, it seems probable that the law arises from something in the very nature of the subject; and the probability is increased by the lesser but still great similarities to be found in the Nullity law of New York. Where Church law differs from either code of civil law, the non-Catholic will not, I trust, assume that the Church is necessarily wrong; unless, indeed, he holds that the civil law is perfect—a highly mystical view, which I have not heard advanced by any lawyer in New York or England.

I should like to express my gratitude to Professor Calamari, of the Fordham University Law School, who read the book in manuscript and made many valuable suggestions on New York Law. I must also thank Mr. Richard O'Sullivan Q.C., who made most valuable comments on what I had to say of English Law.

Needless to say this is not a text-book on Canon Law—the body of laws and regulations the Church issues for the government of her members. The Catholic who has a marriage problem should ask a priest to put him in touch with the Matrimonial Court of the Diocese. If he does not know a priest, a letter to the Bishop will be passed on to an official of the Matrimonial Court.

Contents

Contents

NULLITY OF MARRIAGE

I

Definitions

A. THE NATURE OF MARRIAGE

VERY few single phrases can have wrought so much mischief as the phrase "Marriage is a contract". The man in the street repeats it, without full understanding, knowing nothing of all that goes with it in the mind of the expert; he has never heard of a contract (nor, indeed, is there one) that cannot be brought to an end by the consent of both parties; he therefore argues that marriage, too, since it is a contract, must be terminable in the same way.

If he puts his argument to a lawyer, he gets an answer. The law of England says that marriage is a contract *resulting in a status*;[1] status does not depend upon the will of the citizen, but upon the will of the State. One cannot, without the State's consent, choose a status; one cannot, without the State's consent, vary it. This, from the point of view of English law, disposes of the first argument that marriage, because it is a contract, should be terminable by the consent of the parties; but it still leaves it termina-

[1] Note Apted v. Apted, [1930] P. at p. 260.

3

ble, since status can be varied *by the State*. In New York the wording is different but the effect is the same: as well as the man and woman, the State too is a party and acquires a vested interest when the married status comes into being.

The Catholic Church gives an answer differing only in one word: marriage is a contract resulting not in a status only but in a *relationship*. A man and a woman are free either to make or not to make the agreement to marry. But if they make it, then God attaches certain consequences to their act. To this particular free choice of a man and a woman God has attached the consequence that a real relationship comes into being.

They have stated their will to be husband and wife: God makes them so. This is the sense, and the only sense, of the phrase "marriages are made in heaven"; it does not mean, as those who quote it bitterly or jestingly seem to think, that matches are made in heaven, that God thrusts that man and that woman into each other's arms. The man and the woman make the agreement to marry: God makes the marriage. They are husband and wife by their own consent but by His act.

They are now related to each other—as father to son, or brother to sister, but more closely than either of these—in a relationship directly made by God. "They are no longer two, but one flesh," says Christ Our Lord (Matthew xix.6). Because their oneness is a God-made thing, man cannot alter it: "What God therefore has joined together," Our Lord continues, "let not man put asunder."

God alone can bring a marriage into being; God alone lays down the conditions in which it can cease to be. Once a relationship is in being, the parties cannot alter these conditions; nor can the State; nor can the Church. By God's ordinance, marriage is the lifelong union of a man and a woman for the propagation of the species. Thus, marriage is not terminable, as a contract would be terminable, by the consent of the parties; it is not terminable, as a mere status would be terminable, by the will of the State.

From this it follows that, while the parties can separate, with the husband going to other women, the wife to other men, they are still husband and wife because it was God who made them so; their ignoring of the oneness leaves the oneness untouched: it is beyond their reach, beyond any reach but God's. Similarly a declaration by the State that a husband and wife are no longer husband and wife—a declaration, that is, of divorce—is a mere form of words. The State can *say* that it has broken the marriage-bond between two people; but it has not broken it. During the lifetime of the parties they remain husband and wife; because that is of the nature of marriage as ordained by God.

The failure to understand this teaching of the Catholic Church has given rise to much quite irrelevant argument. Those who urge that the Church should grant, or, at any rate, permit, divorce always do so on the ground that in certain cases it is desirable. But to urge that a thing is desirable is no answer to a statement that it is impossible. And that is the precise truth.

Marriage, then, is a contract resulting in a relationship; better still, it is a relationship resulting from a contract.

For when the relationship comes into being the contract has done its work; it has produced the relationship of marriage, and the parties are now governed in their common life, *not* by the contract (which *they* made), but by the relationship (which *God* made in ratification of their contract).

The principle that, once married, the parties are bound no longer by their agreement but by the nature of marriage, belongs to civil law too. The very word "relation" is used—in a lesser sense than in Catholic doctrine but sometimes coming very close. In a Rhode Island case[2] we find: "Though formed by contract, marriage signifies the relation of husband and wife. . . . When formed this relation is no more a contract than 'fatherhood' or 'sonship' is a contract."

For civil law the relation is not made by God; it is status rather than kinship; but there is the same sense that something has been brought into being that was beyond the power of the parties themselves to produce.

As a practical matter resulting from its being God-made, marriage is not indissoluble just because the parties at their wedding made vows of lifelong fidelity. It is indissoluble because it is marriage.

[2] Ditson v. Ditson, 4 R.I. 87, 101.

The vows are of use as indicating the intention of the parties to marry; but if this intention to marry is shown in some other way without mention of indissolubility, the marriage is still indissoluble; for that is the kind of relation marriage is. There are those who would evade the difficulty by allowing people who do not wish (or feel strong enough for) a permanent union—and who therefore wish to contract a union either for a certain period or terminable if they find that they do not like it—to marry in a registrar's office without vows or promises of lifelong fidelity. This would certainly ensure that any subsequent dissolution of partnership would not be a breach of faith; but only by making the partnership not a marriage at all—because the intention of impermanence contradicts the very nature of marriage. God has taught that the sort of partnership proposed—of a man and a woman living together not married to each other—is sinful.

B. THE DIFFERENCE BETWEEN DIVORCE AND NULLITY

To repeat, marriage is a relationship (God-made) resulting from a contract (man-made). These two terms, relationship and contract, both of them essential to any understanding of marriage, are the subject of two bodies of law: the law of divorce concerns the *relationship*; the law of nullity concerns the *contract*.

The difference between divorce and nullity is therefore about as wide as it is possible to conceive. Divorce claims to break up a marriage actually in being. Nullity means that the marriage never came into being; it is the discovery that the contract to marry did not exist. Marriage is not *only* a contract; but it results from a contract, and if there is no contract no relationship can result.

In any civilized society that treats of marriage at all, there may or may not be a law of divorce; but in *every* civilized society that treats of marriage there is a law of nullity—a law governing the conditions under which the marriage contract is valid. And a moment's thought will show that this must be so, unless either by some odd chance marriage is the one sort of contract about whose validity no subsequent question could ever possibly arise; or else marriage itself is so strange a relationship that any sort of contract—good, bad or indifferent—or even the appearance of a contract, will suffice to bring it into being.

C. NULLITY OF CONTRACT IN GENERAL

Every contract has certain things essential to it simply *as* a contract: many contracts have in addition a number of incidentals, not belonging to contract as such, but attached to this or that particular contract by the authority having jurisdiction in its sphere.

The *essentials* concern the parties and the thing they agree to do:

the parties must be free to make the agreement;
the parties must freely make it;
the thing they agree to do must be lawful in itself.

The *incidentals* may roughly be lumped together as the form or ceremony. In all the more important contracts the authority having jurisdiction insists on some special form.

The absence of an incidental may not be fatal to the contract, but it will be if the law insists upon its presence; thus, an agreement for the sale of land will not in general be enforced by the law of England unless it is in writing and signed; a marriage in England is in general not legally valid if it is not celebrated before an Anglican minister or a registrar.

The absence of an essential *must* be fatal. If a contract is declared null by any court on the ground that one of the essentials was lacking, there is no point in urging that all the incidentals were in order.

In this preliminary discussion it may seem slightly pedantic to point out that an agreement to do one thing does not make a contract to do something different. For example, a court will not consider an agreement to lease a house as a contract to buy it; nor will an agreement of two people to take each other as husband and wife for anything less than their lifetime constitute an agreement to marry—marriage being the union of one man and one woman for life to the exclusion of all others. This is not only the Catholic view. It is a standard definition of English Law. It is stated in a New York case, *Campbell v. Crampton*,[1] which says that marriage is: "the civil *status* of one man and one woman, united in law for life, under the obligation to discharge to each other and to the community those duties *which the community, by its laws, imposes*". The italicized phrase strikes Catholic ears as faintly totalitarian.

[1] 8 Abb NC 363, 2F 417.

II

The Authority of Church and State

I HAVE said that in all civilized societies there must be a law of nullity of marriage, a law by which one may know whether the contract has been entered into or not. A man either is married or he is not: and the civil courts, like the ecclesiastical courts of the Catholic Church, have from time to time to go into the question. There has, of course, to be some appearance of marriage or the question could not arise at all. When it does arise, the general principles upon which the two courts—civil and ecclesiastical—act are very similar. For both courts, the one question is: "Are the parties married to each other?"—that is: "Was there a valid contract?"

Both the State and the Church are concerned with marriage, and both legislate for it. Neither regards it as a mere private arrangement which concerns no one but the parties to it. For, in its very inception, marriage means the addition to society of a new unit, a family; and it adds citizens both to the earthly kingdom and to the Kingdom of God.

Yet neither the State nor the Church is the source from which marriage draws its being or its validity; neither is entitled so to legislate as to alter the nature of marriage. God instituted marriage, and the laws governing its coming into being are His. The State may embody God's laws in its statutes. Further, provided the nature of marriage is not violated, the State may make *incidental* laws to ensure its own objects of peace and orderly government and the general well-being; and such laws are binding. Any laws it may make which violate the nature of marriage—as, for instance, by assuming that it is terminable in the lifetime of the parties—are simply of no effect.

So much for the State's power of legislation. Here we come to a vital distinction between the baptized and the unbaptized. The marriage of the unbaptized is a true relationship which cannot be terminated by any civil or ecclesiastical law; but that of the baptized is, in addition, a sacrament, and this not exceptionally but universally. (The marriage of the unbaptized becomes a sacrament once both are baptized.) The sacrament is not conferred by the priest: the man and the woman are the ministers of the sacrament, conferring it upon each other—this is the one sacrament which priests neither receive nor administer. Two baptized people cannot have the natural relationship only, and exclude the sacrament: for them the two things are inseparable.[1] If two baptized Protestants marry in church or before the registrar, they receive the sacrament though they may never have heard that

[1] See pp. 45–6.

marriage *is* a sacrament. Therefore, since the marriage of the baptized is always a sacrament, it is directly subject to the legislation of the Church: for obviously the question "Are A and B (both of them baptized) married?" is really a question: "Did A and B receive the sacrament of matrimony?"; and to that question only the Church can give an answer—the State is not concerned with sacraments. But in becoming a sacrament marriage does not cease to be marriage, and ecclesiastical law can no more violate its nature than can the laws made by the State.

To summarize, the authority of the Church and State to legislate on marriage is as follows:

(a) Concerning the unbaptized, as I have shown, the State may validly make laws, provided these do not violate the nature of marriage; and if the unbaptized do not observe these State laws their union is null.

(b) Concerning the baptized, the State may validly make laws, provided these do not violate either the nature of marriage or such laws as the Church has laid down in this her own sphere.

(c) Concerning the baptized the Church legislates: but her legislation must not contradict what belongs to the nature of marriage, or what belongs to the nature of sacrament. On both points her rules are rather by way of declaring the truth than of directly legislating. Provided both are safe, she may directly legislate for *all* baptized (*Catholic or not*).

This distinction is to be found in all the Church's teaching on moral questions. The laws made by God for the government of man's soul are not within the Church's power (any more than the laws made by God for the government of man's body). She can declare them with infallible authority, but she does not make them; they are not hers; she has no power over them, and she cannot alter them, or even suspend them. Within the framework, however, of the law of God, the Church has been given by God the power[2] to make what may be regarded as by-laws, and these are binding upon all her subjects.

Concerning the laws of this second sort, two further points may be noted here:

(1) They are her own laws: and therefore (since the laws of any legislature are subject to the authority which makes them) are under her control: she may alter them as seems good to her: for good reason she can dispense individuals from their observance.

(2) They bind *all* the baptized, including non-Catholics, unless these are especially excluded. As an example, consider what has happened about the impediment of disparity of cult—the somewhat dimly-lit term invented by Canon lawyers for the difference between those who are baptized and those who are not. A marriage between a baptized Catholic and an unbaptized person is null, unless the Church has granted a dispensation. Before the new Code of Canon Law was issued in 1918, the impediment applied to all the baptized, non-Catholics as well; but under the New Code these last are excluded from its

[2] E.g., Mt. xvi.19; xviii.18.

effects. In practice, the Church requires for the valid marriage of the *non-Catholic* baptized only that they shall follow the law of their State, and this in all that is not contrary to marriage. If both non-Catholics are baptized, their marriage is a sacrament.

Where two authorities claim to act in the same sphere, there is a strong suspicion (usually justified) that one of them is trespassing. Historically, it is clear that in England the State is the trespasser. For prior to the Reformation, marriage was a matter within the Church's sphere. The State has simply taken it over. But, in any event, the common notion that in obeying the marriage-law of his Church the Catholic is disobeying the law of his country is quite mistaken. The truth is that while both authorities make statements about marriage, the two sets of statements are not so obviously contradictory as one might suppose.

Civil law says, in effect, that a particular union of two people—for example, when one of them is divorced and has a partner living—is not contrary to peace and orderly government and the well-being of society, and fulfils the State's definition of a marriage. The Church says that the same union is harmful to the soul, being contrary to the law of God. Neither is really contradicting the other. Civil law knows nothing of souls, and does not claim any authority to declare the law of God. The State's declaration that a particular union is a marriage in its eyes, is not contradicted by the Church's statement that it is not a marriage in God's. Individual Catholics give respectful attention to their country's view that peace and orderly government do not suffer from such "marriages"; but knowing, from the Church, that the eternal welfare of souls suffers from them, they do not contract them. To tell a Catholic that the law allows them is simply irrelevant, since the Church says they will harm his soul—and the only reassurance civil law can give him on the point is that it knows nothing about that, either way. It is as though a doctor, prescribing for a patient, warned him to avoid roast beef, and the patient retorted that the law allows it.

The Catholic therefore is in no sense a disobedient citizen for believing the Church—on a point where the law does not contradict it. The truth is that Church and State are actually talking about two different things. The Church is talking of marriage—a relation instituted by God and depending on His laws. The State is talking (in effect) of another institution—called, somewhat confusingly, by the same name—owing its validity and its nature not to God but to the will of the State. In England and America, as it happens, the rules governing the State's institution are in many points similar to the rules governing God's: so much so that:

(a) those who contract the God-given relationship usually satisfy the conditions the State lays down for its own institution;

(b) those who enter into the institution recognized by the State usually—though not always—fulfil the conditions laid down by God for His.

In other words the State does not as yet forbid Christians to do what the law of God requires: or force them to do what the law of God forbids.

How long this will continue, no one knows. There are more and more marriages recognized by English and American law which are not marriages in the eyes of God. For the moment, the Church deplores this but need do no more. But if any State legislation tried to force upon Catholics practices repugnant to God's law of marriage (for example, forcing artificial insemination upon the sterile) or to forbid Catholics things demanded by God's law (for example, insisting upon contraception after a given number of children), the Church would be obliged to resist.

The object of this book is simply to set out what the Church's marriage-law is—not to defend it or urge its excellence. But it seems worth while to suggest two considerations bearing on this question of marriage as an institution controlled by the State.

The first is this: if marriage is only a relation drawing its validity from and controlled by the State, then it really ceases to be an *institution*. It becomes something fluctuating and uncertain, varying in meaning and value with the nation's spiritual condition, very much as the French franc varies in meaning and value with the nation's financial credit. Indeed the franc suggests a further comparison, for it fluctuates not only with the nation's credit, but with the Government's; and marriage equally could vary in value not only with some change in the nation's spiritual condition but with a change of government or at the mere whim of a legislator. And it is important that an institution so basic as marriage should be put beyond the reach of those fluctuations and uncertainties which are inseparable from the normal working of human legislators upon subjects which they regard as entirely their own.

The second is more easily stated. All men, when they think of "the State", tend to think of their own State. It may not be irrelevant, therefore, to remind readers that the question whether marriage belongs to the jurisdiction of the Church or the State is not simply a question as between the Church and their own country. The Church is not of one country or of one age. And compared with the marriage-law of—say—Russia in the nineteen-twenties or Afghanistan, even a very determined non-Catholic might prefer that of the Church.

At any rate, we *have* two authorities legislating on marriage: and I propose, in discussing the Church's law of Nullity, to make comparisons with the laws of England and of the State of New York. To repeat what has already been said in the Preface: as this is an essay on the Catholic law of Nullity, the other codes being used only for purposes of comparison, I do not set out the relevant English and American rules with all possible conditions, modifications and exceptions: these are mentioned only if they illustrate either a similarity of approach or a significant difference.

In general the principles are the same in all three codes:

being indeed, for the most part, the application to this rather special problem, of the general law of contract.

The most striking difference arises from the fact that the Church *is* the Church—a religion, and not the religion of the country: the marriage of a priest, for instance, or of a person who has taken solemn vows of chastity, or of a Catholic with one who is not baptized, is null in Church law, valid in English and American law. Other differences lie in the application of principles. These I shall consider as they arise.

Here I wish simply to emphasize that England and New York have a law of nullity, distinct from their law of divorce, and that they draw the same distinction between divorce and nullity that has already been drawn in this book. Where it is decided that a particular matrimonial union is null, both agree with the Church in holding that the parties never were married to each other at all.

III

Grounds of Nullity

NULLITY concerns the contract only: if that is valid, the *relationship* arises and cannot be nullified. Therefore nothing that happens only after the marriage has come into being can possibly be a ground for a decree of nullity. (Since the Matrimonial Causes Act of 1937 there seems to be an exception to this rule in English law, non-consummation being now a ground for nullity. This is discussed later, page 55.) For instance, the fact that the terms of the contract have not been kept seems to many a reason for nullifying it. But the only question asked by Church or State is: "Was the contract properly entered into?" If it was, then there can be no question of nullity. The marriage came into being and the parties are now governed by the laws of marriage, not by the contract: it would simply be untrue, therefore, to say that the union never was a marriage—and that is what a decree of nullity means. At the risk of wearying readers it must be repeated that a decree of nullity does not mean that the marriage has been a failure: it means that the marriage never existed at all: there *was* no marriage to *be* a failure.

Now, to summarize and apply what was said on pages

9 and 10, there may be the appearance of a marriage, yet no real marriage for one of the following reasons:

A. *What was agreed to was not marriage.*

This would mean that there was not even a contract of marriage.

Assuming that the agreement the parties made *was* a contract of marriage, it might still not be a valid contract upon which the relation of marriage would follow, for one of these reasons:

B. *The parties were not free to marry.*
C. *The parties did not agree freely.*

This raises the question of Consent, from which the most difficult Nullity cases arise.

D. *The parties did not observe the due form.*

There are various ways in which the grounds of Nullity may be divided. Here I shall divide them according to these four headings: this division, though not altogether scientifically unexceptionable, is convenient and covers the ground.

A. *Not a contract of marriage:*

the exclusion of some essential element—especially indissolubility, child-bearing, or (for the baptized) the sacrament.

B. *The parties were not free*

    (i) to marry at all:

        already married and husband or wife living

        under age

        Holy Orders

        solemn religious vows

        impotence

    (ii) to marry each other:

        consanguinity

        affinity

        honestas publica

        spiritual relationship

        disparity of cult (one a Catholic, the other not baptized)

        crimen

        abduction

Honestas publica and *crimen* are left in Latin because any English translation would mislead. As far as that goes, the Latin is misleading too: both are labels for a situation too complex to be expressed in one or two words. They will be explained later.

    C. *The parties did not consent:*

        insanity

        ignorance of what marriage is

        ignorance of what the ceremony was

        not the person one thought one was marrying

        force and fear

        condition attached
        simulated consent
D. *Due form not observed:*
        requirements of the appropriate authority not
        met

In this list, those under B, which concern freedom to marry, are called diriment impediments. "Impediment" is from the Latin verb to prevent, "diriment" from the Latin verb to nullify or destroy. The other grounds in the list are not called impediments, because the person is not prevented from making the contract, he simply does not make it. But they are diriment—they destroy; where any one of them is present, there is no marriage.

There are certain other impediments, called impedient or prohibitive, which make a marriage illicit (sinful therefore) but not null. Simple vows (not made in a Religious Order)—for example, a vow not to marry or to become a priest—are of this sort. So is legal adoption where the law of the country makes close relationships arising from it a bar to marriage. So is difference of religion—the difference between a Catholic and a baptized non-Catholic. As this book is on Nullity, these need not be discussed.

Some of the diriment impediments listed above are of divine or natural law—e.g., the exclusion of one of the essentials of marriage, want of consent, impotence, insanity: a man cannot have two wives at a time, marriages in the direct ascending and descending line are impossible. Others—notably disparity of cult, solemn vows, Holy Orders, absence of due form—are of ecclesiastical law, introduced by the Church for the better regulation of marriage but not of its very nature: from them the Church can grant dispensations. Thus the Church could give a dispensation removing the impediment set up by spiritual relationship or by *crimen*, for example, relaxing the restrictions against marriage within some at least of the prohibited degrees, allowing marriage with one who is not baptized, even allowing the marriage of a priest. In some of these instances, dispensations are not uncommon; in others they are rare and altogether extraordinary. All the impediments listed—those of divine law absolutely, the others if no dispensation has been obtained—mean that there is no marriage.

In a general way it may be said that the grounds of Nullity which arise from the nature of man will be found in principle in the law of England and in the law of New York. But there are considerable differences as to what the law of nature actually is—especially with regard to indissolubility and child-bearing and also with regard to the truth that man is not a solitary individual but member of a social order. Some of these differences will be considered later in the book. For both England and New York, the following list will stand:

too close relationship
bigamy

under age (16 in England, 18 in New York)
insanity
impotence
want of understanding
want of consent
want of due form

Both codes make a distinction not found in Church law—at any rate in those terms—between marriages void and marriages voidable.

In England if, for instance, one at least of the parties is under age or officially declared a lunatic, or has a spouse living and undivorced, the marriage is void; on other grounds, marriage is voidable. The distinction is that voidable marriages do, and void marriages do not, require the decision of a court that they are null; though it is usually wise to seek a court decision in any case.

But once a voidable union is declared null by a competent court, it is held to have been void from the beginning. This must not be taken too absolutely: consequences can flow from it. The children of such marriages, as we shall see, are not necessarily illegitimate. In *De Reneville v. De Reneville*[1] (a fascinating case for one who would really study the English Law of Nullity) it was held that, until such a union has been declared null, the domicile of the wife is that of her husband. In this case, as the husband was domiciled in France, it was held that

[1] [1948] P. 100 C.A.

his English wife could not petition in England for nullity on the ground of his impotence. Since the Matrimonial Causes Act of 1950 a wife resident in England for three years can petition in such circumstances.

In New York only incest and bigamy make a marriage void, the rest voidable. The difference is roughly the same as in English law, but in New York a voidable marriage annulled by the courts is, according to the Domestic Relations Law of the State, *void from the date of the court's decision*. Does this mean that it was valid till that moment? If so, then the annulment would be a divorce.

The 1921 case, *Matter of Moncrieff's Will*,[2] holds that the use of the phrase in question in the Revised Statutes (1830) was not intended to alter the rule applied by courts of Equity that duress and fraud, once proved, made a marriage void from the beginning, and that in effect it meant only that the marriage must be *held* valid until the court had acted. But such cases as *Sleicher v. Sleicher*[3] and *Gaines v. Jacobsen*[4] raise, without settling, the question whether this is so.

The two cases deal with a roughly similar set of facts. A wife has divorced her first husband, with an agreement that she be paid a fixed income unless and until she marries again. The woman does marry again and the allowance ceases. The second union is annulled. In the first case, the allowance was restored, but only from the date

[2] 235 NY 390.
[3] 251 NY 366.
[4] 308 NY 216.

of the annulment. In the second case the allowance was not restored at all! The reason for the difference was that in between the two cases, the law made it possible for the wife to get alimony after an annulment. Both cases were settled, in fact, not on the question of when an annulled marriage becomes void, but on the entirely practical principle that a woman should not be entitled to support from two men at the same time!

The opinion is ventured by a stranger to New York Law that, in general, the annulment of a voidable marriage means that the union never was a marriage; yet that it was not a mere nothing either, not what lawyers call a "fornicatious union", but a real partnership from which certain results flow (under section 1140 A. of the Civil Practice Act, for example, a woman whose marriage has thus been annulled, may, as we have just seen, get alimony).

In Canon Law there is something similar to the distinction between void and voidable. Generally no marriage can be treated as null until two Church courts have declared it so; but some unions are so obviously null—the attempted marriage of a priest, for example, or of a person with a spouse living, or of a Catholic in a registrar's office—that one decision is enough. The Court of the Diocese settles these matters, as also where the relationship is too close—by blood or affinity or spiritual relation—or where a Catholic has married an unbaptized person without a dispensation (see Canon 1990).

But in all other cases there must be two hearings and two decisions in favour of nullity. In the Diocesan Court, the ecclesiastical court of first instance, there is an official called the Defensor Vinculi—the Defender of the Marriage Bond—a sort of devil's advocate against nullity. If the Diocesan Court says the marriage is null, the Defender of the Bond must appeal, either to the Court of the Archdiocese or the Rota, the Court in Rome which treats of marriage cases. Even if the second decision is in favour of nullity, the Defender of the Bond may—if his conscience tells him, in spite of all, that this *is* a real marriage—ask for another trial, by different judges of the Rota.

All this is a reminder that the Church does not take nullity lightly. Where there is certainty, a decree is given. But where there is no certainty, it is not: "marriage", says Canon Law, "enjoys the favour of the law; when in doubt, a marriage is to be considered valid until the contrary is proved" (Canon 1014). Clearly a social order in which marriages could be lightly broken would be a chaos. But in his Allocution of October 1941, Pius XII explained that this is to be understood only as requiring that the invalidity be proved with moral certainty—not, in other words, the sort of proof which excludes all imaginable or conceivable doubt. The Pope explained the reason why moral certainty is sufficient: "If the parties are not in reality bound by any existing bond of marriage, they are entitled by natural law to contract marriage."

RESTRICTION ON THE GUILTY

We have just noted the statement of Pope Pius XII that an ecclesiastical tribunal has no right or power to demand more than moral certainty of the invalidity of a marriage; and we have noted the reason he gives— namely that those whose union is not in fact a marriage are entitled by natural law to marry. But the Church treats one class of people as having laid themselves open to being denied this natural right. The party who was the guilty cause of the alleged nullity of a marriage cannot petition for a declaration of its nullity.[5]

Thus he is in a curious position: he may be unmarried, but he is debarred from establishing the fact in the eyes of the Church, and so cannot contract a valid marriage. In other words, to have guiltily impeded one's first marriage is like a kind of diriment impediment, not directly invalidating one's second marriage, but preventing the declaration of the nullity of the first, so that the second cannot take place. This is the price a person must pay, the penalty inflicted upon him by the Church, for his wrong-doing in the contracting of the first union. The regulation is intended also to safeguard, as far as is possible, the rights of the wronged party to the union.

Note that this restriction applies only to one who was the *guilty* cause of the impediment or other ground of

[5] Sacred Congregation of the Sacraments, *Provida Mater Ecclesia*, 15 August 1936, *Acta Apostolicae Sedis*, pp. 28–313.

nullity; one who did not know he was acting wrongly would not be affected.

So the guilty party cannot himself petition for nullity. But he may place the facts before an official of the diocese called the Promoter of Justice. And it is open to this official to challenge the validity of the marriage himself.

If the ground on which the validity is impugned is defective consent—a positive act of the will excluding marriage, for example, or excluding some essential characteristic of marriage—then the Promoter of Justice must not at once bring suit for nullity, but must urge the parties to make a true act of consent, thus validating the original union.

Whether the ground is defective consent or some other, the Promoter of Justice may himself decide, as we have said, to challenge the validity of the union. The conditions for his doing so are set out in the Instructions from the Sacred Congregation of Sacraments from which we have been quoting; it would be difficult to explain them clearly in the space of this book—anyone concerned should consult a priest, who will put him in touch with the appropriate authorities.

VALIDATION OF MARRIAGE

Where the impediment which rendered a marriage invalid has ceased, all that is needed is a renewal of consent.

If the impediment is publicly known, the consent must be renewed before a priest and two witnesses; if it is known only to the parties, the consent may be renewed privately; if it is known to one only of the parties, then it is sufficient if that one renews consent.

Related to this is the *sanatio in radice*. This is too large a matter for full discussion here. An example must suffice. If a Catholic goes through a form of marriage with a non-Catholic in a registry office, the normal way of validating the marriage would be to go through the correct form before a priest. But, if this would be impossible or seriously inconvenient, the Holy See can grant a *sanatio in radice* without requiring any official act of any kind, even without the knowledge of the non-Catholic party, provided that there is reasonable assurance that the faith of the Catholic spouse or of the children is in no danger. The effect is to make the marriage valid "in its root": it is as if it had been valid from the beginning. The children born of it are legitimate.

When there is urgent danger of death, marriages may be validated by the bishop of the diocese (or the pastor if the bishop cannot be got in time) provided that the impediment is of ecclesiastical law; but this does not apply if the impediment is priesthood or affinity in the direct line. Where the marriage is thus validated, any children are legitimated.

IV

What Was Agreed To
Was Not Marriage

By this is meant that the man and woman made an agreement, only it was an agreement, not to marry, but to enter into some other form of union. Marriage is essentially the permanent union of a man and a woman for the propagation of the species. Any condition made by the parties that contradicts one of the essentials of the marriage relationship means that they are not contracting to marry, and from an agreement so conditioned no marriage can result.

(i) Exclusion of Permanence

The most obvious instance of this is where the man and the woman explicitly agree that their marriage shall be terminated either at the end of a particular period, or if either of them should demand it. This is not an agreement to marry—since marriage is the union of a man and a woman *for life*. If it can be proved that such a condition was made, the Church has no choice in the matter: there was no contract to marry, therefore no marriage resulted. The adequacy of the ceremony, the number of children, the years of life together—none of these things can alter the fact that the parties were not married.

This was the ground on which the *Marconi Case* was decided. I summarize the account given in the *Acta Apostolicae Sedis* (1927, p. 217):

> Guglielmo Marconi in 1903 met and proposed to Beatrice O'Brien. She refused him. The following year they met again. He proposed and was accepted. Her relations—particularly her mother—did not welcome the match, as it seemed to them that she was not sufficiently in love to live happily with him for the rest of her life. Her mother consented to the marriage only on his promising not to oppose her seeking a divorce if the marriage turned out unhappily. On this condition *sine qua non*—accepted by Beatrice O'Brien—the marriage was celebrated, in March 1905, before an Anglican minister; for though Signor Marconi had been born of a Catholic father and baptized in the Catholic faith, he had been brought up by his mother as a Protestant, and was in fact an Anglican at the time of the marriage.
>
> They lived together—"though neither continuously, nor always in the harmony becoming to husband and wife"—till 1918. Then they separated, and Signor Marconi later secured a divorce on the ground of her adultery. In 1924 he petitioned for a decree of nullity from the Diocesan Court at Westminster on the ground that the condition made be-

tween them at the time the marriage was solemnized was contrary to the nature of marriage. Evidence of the existence of the condition was given by the two parties, by the brother and sister of Beatrice O'Brien, and by Marchio Solari, a friend of Signor Marconi.

The petition was successful in the Archdiocese of Westminster, and later before the Rota: such a condition (if actually a *condition* and not merely an erroneous belief that marriage might safely be entered into since it was dissoluble) means that the state the parties agreed to enter was *not* marriage.

Observe the phrase in brackets. In a 1918 case[1] the law was laid down as follows: a mere erroneous belief that marriage is dissoluble (even if this is the law of the State or sect to which a person belongs) does not invalidate the contract *even if without that erroneous belief the contract would not have been made*. But if—and only if—by positive and explicit act one party says he wishes to contract a dissoluble marriage, then no marriage results.

More recent cases seem to make rather less strict demands. It is still held that a mere erroneous belief that marriage can be dissolved does not nullify. But a positive act of the will excluding indissolubility (or children or fidelity) does, even if not made into an explicit condition. This is brought out clearly in a decision of the Rota of 23 March 1956.[2] The marriage under consideration had

---

[1] DeLeffert and Bartels, *Acta Apostolicae Sedis*, 1918, p. 215.
[2] Reported in Bouscaren, *Digest of Canon Law*, vol. iv, p. 332.

taken place in the Church of Mount Carmel in the Vicariate Apostolic of Alexandria. Two children died in infancy. From 1940 to 1945 the man was a prisoner in a concentration camp, and the woman got a civil decree of separation. The man asked for and received a decree of nullity on the ground that the woman had not intended the marriage to be indissoluble. The Rota held that a marriage is invalidated not only by an *absolute* exclusion of indissolubility but also by its *hypothetical* exclusion —a positive act of the will that if certain things happen dissolution will be sought; that in this case the evidence made it clear that the woman's views on the matter at the time of the marriage were not merely speculative but practical, not merely about marriage as such but about her own marriage; and that she was so convinced of her right to divorce that she was quite incapable of abandoning her conviction.

Where one party has the intention of contracting a terminable marriage without explicitly making it a condition, there is one immediate question for the ecclesiastical court. Can the existence of this intention (at the time of the marriage of course) be proved? Clearly if a person had such an intention and never communicated it to anybody, the court could not act upon it. But provided the intention can be proved, the marriage will be declared null.

So marriage is null where there is a positive intention to terminate *if*—. Earlier the Rota had perhaps gone a little further: on a first hearing it refused a decree of nullity, but on a second hearing granted it, in a case where a man had reserved to himself the right to divorce.

What of non-Catholics living in a society where divorce is so frequent as to be almost commonplace? It seems probable that many of them no longer regard marriage in itself as indissoluble. What matters, however, is not what they think about the institution of marriage, but what they intend about their own marriage. Only if they can be shown to have positively intended a terminable marriage for themselves—absolutely or conditionally—is their union not a marriage.

There is probably as yet no Western country in which divorce is so much a matter of course that it can be presumed that those who marry in a registrar's office do so with no intention of permanence. But there are countries in which things seem to be moving that way—at least towards a point at which the onus of proof is on one who asserts the validity of such a marriage and not, as at present, on those who deny it.

A careful reading of the two cases quoted will show the meaning of the rule that an agreement to contract any but a lifelong and exclusive union is not an agreement to marry, and that therefore a marriage cannot result from it. The same principle holds in English law. In *Hyde v. Hyde and Woodmansee*,[3] a case in England concerning the marriage in 1858 of two Mormons in Salt Lake City, marriage was defined as "the voluntary union for life of one man and one woman to the exclusion of

[3] 1 P. & D. 130

all others". A leading case in which this definition is applied is In re *Bethell, Bethell v. Hildyard.*[4]

Bethell married Teepoo, a native woman, in South Africa; the wedding was celebrated with all the rites of her tribe; they lived together as husband and wife till he was killed; ten days later a child was born. In a document signed by him in 1883, he made some provision for the woman, and the child that might be born, out of the proceeds of sale of property owned by him in the colony. The English Court held that the union was a marriage not in the Christian but in the Baralong sense; that the Baralong tribe allowed polygamy; that consequently this was not a valid marriage, since according to the law of England marriage is the "voluntary union for life of one man and one woman to the exclusion of all others".

I quote from the judgment (p. 235):

"The evidence clearly proves that *Christopher Bethell intended* that the relationship between himself and Teepoo should at least be that of husband and wife in the sense in which those terms are used among the Baralongs. That relationship, however, is essentially different from that which bears the same name in Christendom, for the Baralong husband is at liberty to take more than one wife. . . . I

[4] 38 Ch. D. 220.

think that the proper inference is that *he meant* to enter into no higher or other union than that which between members of the tribe was regarded as a marriage . . . *there is nothing to show that Teepoo regarded herself* as entering into any other union than such as prevails among the tribe to which she belongs."

I have italicized certain phrases which are of the utmost significance (though, as it chances, some of the legal text-books appear to have overlooked them). The marriage was null in English law not simply because of the custom of polygamy among the Baralongs but because the *intention of the parties* was to contract the ordinary Baralong marriage, and such a marriage, since it is not the exclusive union of a man and a woman for life, is not what English law regards as a marriage at all.

A later case bearing closely on this point is *Nachimson v. Nachimson*[5]; it is worth examination because its statement of the principle is even clearer.

This was the trial of an issue whether the parties to a suit for judicial separation had ever been husband and wife (as understood by English law).

They had been married in 1924 in Moscow under the Soviet law of 1918. In 1929 the marriage was dissolved, according to Russian law as it was then (but is not now), by the man's simply giving notice

[5] [1930] P. 217, C.A.

of dissolution at the Russian consulate-general in Paris: by Russian law marriage could be terminated by the desire of one party, and no judge or registrar had any option but to record the dissolution. On the first hearing in England, Mr. Justice Hill decided that the union was not a marriage as understood by the law of England, since it was terminable by the desire of the parties. On appeal this decision was reversed, and the Russian marriage held to be a valid marriage as understood in English law; on the ground that the civil law providing for dissolution was not part of the marriage contract, and that the condition of dissolution did not depend upon any prior agreement between the parties—in fact, they could not escape from that condition, since it was in the law of their country; and they could not have done more than they did to acquire the status of husband and wife. The woman stated in evidence that when she had married, she had intended the union to be for life, and there was no evidence that the man had intended otherwise.

It seems that the decision given by the English Court of Appeal in this case would equally have been given by the Rota. As Lord Justice Lawrence said, any other decision "would entail the strange consequence that no valid marriage would have been possible in Russia whilst the relevant Russian law was in force . . . however much (the parties) might have desired to get married or to enter into a union for life".

In short, a State cannot make marriage impossible for its subjects merely by itself holding a view of marriage which is not the Christian view. The question must always be, not "What did the State think about marriage?", but "What did the parties intend?" This principle governed the decisions in In re *Bethell*, in *Nachimson v. Nachimson*, and in more recent English cases where nullity—claimed on the ground that Russian marriages were invalid because Russian Law does not regard living together as of their essence—was refused. It is an absolute principle of Church Law. On it the *Marconi Case* was decided.

For English law, the definition of marriage as "the union of one man and one woman for life to the exclusion of all others" encounters a certain difficulty from the existence of a law of divorce. English courts have, of course, held that the *possibility* of divorce is not contrary to the definition, but they have never been called upon to decide the precise question at issue in the *Marconi Case:* "Would a *condition* of divorce made prior to or at the time of the marriage-contract be sufficient to prevent the definition of marriage from being fulfilled and so make the marriage null?" But though English courts have never had to *decide* the point, all three judges in the case of *Nachimson v. Nachimson* expressed opinions which seem to suggest that such a prior condition would (as the Church courts held) invalidate the marriage. The clearest statement was made by Lord Justice Romer:

"None of these difficulties arise except upon the

somewhat cynical hypothesis[6] that parties intend to contract marriage, not for life but only until its dissolution. Lord Brougham regarded the intention of the parties as going to the root of the matter, and for myself, I prefer to consider each of the two persons contracting marriage *in this country* as intending to be bound to one another for life rather than as intending to be bound until the other one commits adultery."

As I have said, the point at issue in the *Marconi Case* has not arisen in an English court, or indeed, in a New York court as far as I can find. In a 1940 case, *Delfino v. Delfino*,[7] the parties went much further in ruling out anything that could be called marriage—the girl persuaded the man to go through a form of marriage "to protect her name", promising that they would not live together as husband and wife and that she would release him by petitioning for divorce or nullity (she to pay half the expenses!). In fact she did not keep either promise. In the end it was the man who sued for nullity but was refused it—not because the Court thought theirs was a real marriage—simply on the ground that "the conduct of the parties constituted a farce and cannot be countenanced". To give the nullity sought "would open the door to trial or companionate marriage". In 1952 *Amsden v. Amsden*[8] was a somewhat similar case, but with no cohabitation and the nullity was given.

[6] Who knows how long this hypothesis will seem cynical?
[7] 35 NYS 2d 693.
[8] 110 NYS 2d 307.

In both cases it was taken for granted that an agreement which excludes essentials does not make a marriage. But in both the exclusion was far greater than in the *Marconi Case.* As I have said, neither English nor New York courts have had to decide a case quite like it. But whatever decision would actually be given in these courts—which have to make allowance for the fact that civil law allows divorce—there can be only one decision for a Church court which holds divorce to be impossible. An agreement for a temporary union (however that union is to be terminated) is not an agreement to marry.

(*ii*) *Exclusion of Children*

There is, however, another form of the general principle that marriage will result only from an agreement to *marry:* if the parties explicitly agree that they will invariably practise contraception, then they are agreeing to something that contradicts the very nature of marriage.

The primary object of the institution of marriage is the procreation of children. An agreement which has the prevention of procreation as its *direct* object is, therefore, not an agreement to marry; and such a condition, if proved, is ground for nullity in the law of the Church. If, in spite of all precautions, the woman was found to have conceived, there would still be no marriage because what she intended involved a denial of marriage's essential nature.

It is to be noted that the Church allows the marriage

of people who cannot have children—by reason of age, for instance—because it is not by their will that the primary purpose of marriage is excluded, and the secondary reasons—companionship, the use of their physical powers, and the development of each personality by the other—can still operate.

What English law would say about all this was, until recently, uncertain. No act of Parliament says what marriage is; and the definition adopted by the courts did not help—for, oddly enough, while it described marriage as the union of a man and a woman for life, by a certain pleasing prudishness it omitted to say what the object of the union was: it did not even say what the nature of the union was. Two decisions in the forties shed light—conflicting light; but as the second was a decision of the House of Lords (the court of ultimate appeal in such cases) it won the conflict, as far as English courts are concerned. The question at issue in each case was not the validity of the marriage agreement, but whether the use of contraceptives meant that the marriage was not consummated.

In the first case, *Cowen v. Cowen,*[9] the Court of Appeal decided that it meant exactly that, on the ground that one of the chief ends of marriage is the procreation of children; and this is intentionally frustrated both by the use of contraceptives and by *coitus interruptus.*

In *Baxter v. Baxter*[10] the House of Lords took the op-

[9] (1945) Times Law Review; reversed in [1946] P. 36 (C.A.).
[10] [1948] A.C. 274.

posite view (at least as regards contraception). Lord
Jowett said he saw no reason to hold that procreation of
children is the principal end of marriage: "In any view
of Christian marriage the essence of the matter is that
the children, if there be any, should be born into a family,
as that word is understood in Christendom generally;
and in the case of spouses of a particular faith that they
should be brought up and nurtured in that faith."

New York law does regard the carrying on of the race
as an end of marriage. A Catholic canonist could hardly
have put it more strongly than it was put in the case of
Amsterdam v. Amsterdam,[11] where marriage is described
as "a mutual and voluntary compact . . . suitably ratified,
to live together as husband and wife until death, with the
object of constituting a family for the preservation of
moral and social purity, the continuance of the race, and
the propagation of children and their nurture, training
and preparation for family welfare and the general good
of society."

All the same, the intention to have no children would
not of itself make a marriage void by New York law.
But the refusal to have them might be a cause for annulment as fraud—on the ground that, if nothing is said
in advance by one party about excluding children, the
other would be entitled to assume that a reasonable
effort would be made to have them. In the 1943 case
Schulman v. Schulman[12] the judge said that if nothing

[11] 56 NY Supp 2d 19.
[12] 180 Misc 904, 46 NY Supp 2d 158.

had been said between the parties before the marriage took place, "the silence of the wife warrants the inference that she intends to enter into marriage with all the usual implications, including willingness to have children". Her insistence, after marriage, that she was entitled to decide *when* she should have a child "injects into the contract a provision the law does not place there—a mental reservation affecting a vital element in the marriage contract". The judge refers to *Mirizio v. Mirizio*[13] (which will be glanced at later in a different connection) where the judge who gives the majority decision says that refusal of cohabitation "strikes at the very basic obligations arising from the marriage contract", because cohabitation "is the basis upon which must rest the perpetuation of society and civilization . . . if it is not to be maintained that we have the alternative either of no children or illegitimate children, and the State abhors either result". The marriage was annulled on the ground of fraud. (The question of fraud will be discussed later; it plays a considerable part in New York nullity cases.)

(iii) *Exclusion of the Sacrament*

It has been said earlier that, for two baptized people, marriage is a sacrament: they cannot have the one without the other. A definite condition excluding one excludes the other. Obviously if, as a result of any of the conditions already mentioned, the *marriage* does not come into being, then there is no sacrament. Equally, if

[13] 242 NY 74, 150 NE 605, 44 ALR 74.

there is a definite condition or a definite intention to exclude the *sacrament*, then the sacrament *is* excluded, and there is no marriage. Observe that marriage is a sacrament not only for two baptized Catholics marrying before a Catholic priest, but for any two baptized people marrying in their own Church or in a registrar's office. The fact that they do not know that marriage is a sacrament does not prevent their receiving it. Nothing would do that save a deliberate resolve to exclude the sacrament—a resolve they are hardly likely to make given their unawareness that marriage *is* a sacrament. But if they do make that resolve, they do not receive the sacrament nor are they married. To exclude one of two inseparables is always to exclude the other.

The moral of all this section is that no power on earth can prevent people making an invalid marriage if they wish to do so, because it is they—the parties, not the Church, and not the State—who make the contract. The contract is what their agreement makes it; and there is no way of preventing people omitting something essential or adding something fatal, so that the contract they make is not a contract of marriage. The Church teaches that people who live together in a union thus invalidated are living in sin, unmarried. If she knows of the condition beforehand, she can forbid the marriage and refuse to solemnize it; but if they do not tell her of the condition, she can do nothing about it. Nor can anyone else.

V

The Parties Were Not Free
To Marry

UNDER this heading come almost all the cases which have
no place in civil law, though on the whole they present
no difficulty to the ordinary English or American mind.
For convenience they may be divided into:

(a) cases where one or other of the parties is not
free to marry anyone;

(b) cases where the parties are not free to marry
each other.

A. WHERE ONE OR OTHER OF THE
PARTIES IS NOT FREE TO
MARRY ANYONE

(i) Spouse Living

The most obvious case is where one of the parties already has a wife or husband living. This is common to
both Church law and English law. Neither will allow a

man to have two wives or a woman two husbands, at the same time.

A problem arises where one of them has been married before, and has reason to think the first partner is dead, but cannot prove it. In English law if one partner is absent for seven years continuously, and has not been heard of by the other, then the other may marry again without risk of being found guilty of bigamy. But if the original party happens to be alive, he is still the true husband, and the second ceremony is not a marriage. Since the Matrimonial Causes Act of 1950, it is permissible for anyone domiciled in England, whose partner has thus vanished and who has good ground for thinking the partner dead, to approach the court; and if the grounds are found reasonable—which may mean at a minimum that the petitioning party has made the enquiries possible in the circumstances—the court may make a decree allowing death to be presumed and dissolving the marriage. Once the decree is made absolute, even the reappearance of the absent partner does not affect the validity of the second marriage.

In Church law absence alone, even long absence, does not give rise to a presumption of death: there must be some evidence that the missing partner has died. But it need not be absolutely conclusive—it will suffice if the accounts of witnesses, for example, or the circumstances in which the missing person was last heard of, convince the appropriate Church authorities. If the party presumed dead is not dead, then the original marriage still stands and the second union is not marriage: for the man and woman to cohabit after the discovery that the first partner was alive after all would be the sin of adultery.

New York also has a rule that a person who has been sentenced to imprisonment for life—or sentenced to death, with commutation to imprisonment for life—is civilly dead and the un-imprisoned spouse can remarry, thus terminating the first marriage.

English law complicates its own rule that no one can have two spouses at once by allowing divorce and re-marriage. But even here the divorced parties must tread warily: if one of them marries again before the divorce decree is made absolute, the second marriage is void.

It may be worth mentioning here the view, not of the Church of England but of some Anglicans, that the "innocent" party in a divorce who re-marries should be allowed to receive communion, just as though he or she were truly married. There is confused thinking here. Civil divorce either terminates a marriage or it does not. If it does, then there is no problem about either party marrying again: innocent of the cause of divorce or guilty, each is now single. But if civil divorce does not terminate a marriage, then husband and wife are still husband and wife: if the "innocent" party marries again— the wife let us say, for gallantry—she has two husbands; and however innocent she may have been of the original adultery or desertion or cruelty (or whatever the cause of divorce was) she is now guilty of the sin of bigamy, she is living with a man to whom she is not married.

In New York, if a marriage ends in divorce, the party in whose favour the divorce is granted is free to marry again when the decree has been made final; but the one against whom it is granted cannot remarry without the permission of the court, which will not be granted till three years have passed, and not then without evidence of good conduct.

New York law also differs from Church law and English law by not holding absolutely that a person can have only one spouse at a time. Reading the cases, one does not easily discover a clear principle. Where death has been wrongly presumed and the former partner is alive, where divorce in another state is not recognized by New York so that the former marriage is still valid there, the courts are unwilling to grant a decree of nullity to the advantage of one who has behaved badly. They give the impression sometimes of acting not upon any view of what marriage is but from a natural instinct against letting villains profit by their villainy—which is not unlike the line the Church takes in not allowing the party who is the guilty cause of the impediment to challenge the validity of the marriage (see page 29). More profoundly the principle is the one brought out in the court's refusal to terminate the Delfino marriage (see page 41)—namely that it would be against the common good to allow people to make a travesty of the law and get away with it. New York regards the common good as having a bearing on whether a marriage should or should not be declared null, of which there is hardly a trace in English law, apart from the feeling that marriages should not lightly be declared null. The common good affects the *status* of marriage once it is contracted, but in the question whether the contract was validly made practically everything depends in English law on what the man and woman did and intended.

In one New York case the man lived with the woman for *ten years after he knew* that the former husband, presumed dead, was still alive; he then sued for nullity and did not get it.

There are interesting cases on unrecognized divorce. In one, the man paid the costs of a woman's Nevada divorce, knowing that New York would not admit it; he married her, sued for nullity on this ground, and failed to get it. In another, the man arranged and paid for the woman's divorce and married her *before the divorce was final* in order to escape induction into the armed forces: he tried for nullity and failed. In recent cases the nullity has been granted in these circumstances, but the man has been forced to pay alimony.

(ii) Age

Common to all three codes is the principle of a minimum age—sixteen for boys, fourteen for girls in Church law.

In English law the rule has changed. Till 1929, if either party was under seven, the marriage was void; if the boy was under fourteen or the girl under twelve, either could confirm or repudiate the marriage on reaching fourteen or twelve. The Age of Marriage Act of 1929 makes the marriage void if either is under sixteen.

In New York a marriage is voidable if either is under the age of eighteen. Before the Domestic Relations Law of 1922, a marriage was null if either party was under the legal age (even if the parents had consented). But now the court will consider the facts of the case and decide accordingly; if the too young party continues to cohabit after reaching the legal age, there will be no voiding of the marriage.

(*iii* and *iv*) *Holy Orders* and *Solemn Religious Vows*

Peculiar to Church law are the impediments of *ordo* and *votum,* which render invalid the marriage of men in Holy Orders (from and above the rank of subdeacon), and of those who have taken Solemn Vows of poverty, chastity and obedience in a religious order. There is nothing equivalent to this in English law, but a non-Catholic can understand their consistency in a Church which forbids the marriage of priests and recognizes solemn vows of chastity. These two impediments are of ecclesiastical law and the Church can, therefore, dispense from them. It seldom does so even for those who have not gone beyond subdiaconate or diaconate. Dispensation to marry is very rare indeed for those who have been ordained priest and is never given to one who has been consecrated bishop. (A *simple* religious vow of chastity, i.e. one not made publicly, does not make a marriage null but illicit only, save in the case of certain religious orders.)

This may be a convenient place to mention a ground of nullity in English law which is not one in the law of the Church. By the Royal Marriage Act, if any descendant of George II (other than the offspring of princesses who have married foreigners) wishes to marry without the consent of the reigning sovereign, he cannot do so unless, being over twenty-five, he gives the Privy Council a year's notice of his intention; and even then he cannot marry if both Houses of Parliament express disapprobation. If any such person goes through the form of marriage in defiance of these provisions, the marriage is held by English law to be null and void.

(v) Impotence

In all three codes, the impotence of the other party (not for generation, but for intercourse) is a ground for nullity.

The question of impotence is too complex, legally and medically, for detailed treatment here. In a general way, all three codes are agreed that only inability to have intercourse is a ground for nullity. Inability to procreate children, whether through age or some physical defect, does not render a marriage void. (In a New York case it was decided that incapacity for intercourse is no ground of nullity if the parties were old at the time of the marriage—the defendant was sixty-nine.) To render a marriage null, impotence need not be general; it is sufficient if one party is impotent with regard to the other (which may be a purely psychological incapacity).

In Church law the condition must be shown to be either absolutely incurable, or curable only by a dangerous operation. This is roughly the law of New York also, but it is no longer a requirement of English law. In one case,[1] the Roman Rota gave a decree of nullity where intercourse was rendered possible to the husband only by the taking of aphrodisiacs which deprived him, for the time being, of the use of reason.

New problems have arisen since the coming into use of artificial insemination. Quite apart from the morality of this, Pius XII, in an Allocution of 29 September, 1949,[2] states that it does not remove the impediment of impotence. In his Address to the Midwives, 29 October, 1951,[3] the Pope taught that the union in one flesh of which Our Lord spoke does not mean the union of two life germs, which can be brought about artificially, but of two persons.

In an English case,[4] a nullity was granted on the ground that the husband's incapacity for complete intercourse was not remedied by artificial insemination even with his own seed. (It is thought by a leading English authority[5] that artificial insemination with seed from a third person might not be held adultery because there

---

[1] Bouscaren III, 273–4.
[2] *Acta Apostolicae Sedis*, pp. 41–55.
[3] *Acta Apostolicae Sedis*, pp. 43–835.
[4] R.E.L. v. E.L. (1949), p. 211.
[5] Latey, p. 77.

was no bodily contact—an argument not unrelated to what the Pope said about union in one flesh. The same author reminds us that the use of a third party as donor might mean that he was the father, by different mothers, of children who, not knowing that he was their father, might marry each other incestuously.)

A careful distinction must be drawn between the nullity of a marriage on account of impotence and the dissolution of a marriage on account of non-consummation. The conditions in which a non-consummated marriage can be dissolved by the Pope are discussed in Chapter VIII. To summarize—impotence is a ground for nullity in all three laws: non-consummation is a ground for dissolution in Church law but not in English law; until recently non-consummation was not by itself a ground for nullity in any of the three codes, since is arises after the marriage. But since the Matrimonial Causes Act of 1937, non-consummation has been a ground for nullity in English law. And where there is non-consummation New York courts frequently decide for a nullity which they would not have granted had there been intercourse.

B. WHERE THE PARTIES WERE NOT FREE TO MARRY EACH OTHER

It is the rule of all three codes, though with differences of detail into which we need not enter here, that a marriage is null if the parties are too closely related. The relationship may be blood-relationship (consanguinity) or relationship by marriage (affinity).

(*i*) *Blood-Relationship*

In the direct line of ascent and descent, marriage is never permissible. A man cannot marry any ancestress or any descendant, whether legitimate or not.

In the collateral line—brothers and sisters (whether of the whole or half blood) cannot marry one another, nor can first cousins or second cousins. Uncles cannot marry nieces, or aunts nephews.

(*ii*) *Affinity*

By marriage (consummated or not) each partner becomes related to the other's blood-relations, though of course the relations of one are not related to the relations of the other. But the impediment of affinity (New York law knows nothing of it) is absolute only in the line of ascent and descent: a man cannot marry his dead wife's mother or grandmother or her daughter or grand-daughter. In the collateral line the impediment extends only as far as first cousins—a man cannot marry his dead wife's sister, aunt, niece, or first cousin. (All these impediments are listed for the man, they apply to the same degrees of relationship for the woman.)

For both blood-relationship and relationship by marriage, dispensations can be obtained. In the direct line of consanguinity they are never granted; a dispensation for the marriage of an uncle and niece would be granted only for very strong reasons. Dispensations are granted from the impediment of affinity in the collateral line, but rarely in the direct line—if a man wanted to marry his dead wife's daughter by a previous marriage, for instance.

The impediment of affinity gave rise to the most important nullity case in English history. Henry VIII, whatever his limitations as a theologian may have been, was not so ill-instructed as to think that he could secure a divorce. What he sought was a decree of *nullity*, on the ground that he had married his deceased brother's wife, Katherine of Aragon.[6] Pope Julius II had given a dispensation for Henry's marriage. There was a good deal of argument, of which the relevance is not obvious (since affinity arises from marriage whether consummated or not) as to whether the marriage with Arthur had ever been consummated—Katherine said it had not. In any case Henry saw that his only chance was to show that Julius II's dispensation did not remedy the impediment. His first idea was to deny the Pope's power to give a dispensation in such a case. The Church can legislate on marriage, provided the God-given nature of marriage is not infringed; the Pope can dispense, therefore, from any impediment that is not of divine institution. To show that Julius had no power to grant this dispensation, Henry would have had to show that marriage with a de-

[6] See Constant, *La Réforme en Angleterre*.

ceased brother's wife was contrary to divine law. Obviously it is not; and his only hope, therefore, was to show that the dispensation was invalid, through some irregularity of form. This too failed. How Henry to cut that small knot cut a greater one the whole world knows.

(*iii*) *Public Decency* (honestas publica)

Affinity arises only from marriage. But the Church has established another impediment arising from sexual unions other than marriage. If two people have lived together—either in an invalid marriage (consummated or not) or in a liaison publicly known—it is regarded as an affront to public decency for either to marry the parent or grandparent, child or grandchild, of the other.

The next three impediments belong to Church Law only. So indeed does the one following them, abduction, though England and New York might declare marriages void on its account as preventing free consent.

(*iv*) *Spiritual Relationship*

This arises from baptism. The recipient of baptism cannot marry either a godparent or the person who performed the baptism. (For readers unfamiliar with Catholic teaching, it may be worth mentioning that it is not only priests who baptize. In case of emergency *anyone* may baptize—man or woman or child.)

(v) *Difference of Cult*

"Disparitas cultus" is the technical name for the difference between one who is baptized and one who is not. (It should not be confused with *mixta religio*—the difference between a Catholic and a baptized non-Catholic.) As we have already noted, the impediment of difference of cult no longer applies to baptized non-Catholics unless they were at one time members of the Church—either having been baptized in it or converted to it for a time. But Catholics, in this wide sense, cannot validly marry an unbaptized person unless they obtain a dispensation.

The conditions on which a dispensation is given are the same as for *mixed marriage* (see Chapter VII). The non-Catholic must promise, among other things, that any children of the marriage shall be brought up as Catholics. If it is proved that the promises were not meant when they were given, then the dispensation is null, the impediment of difference of cult remains, and the marriage is null. A similar insincerity would not invalidate a mixed marriage, since *mixta religio* is not a *diriment* impediment. When a mixed marriage is null it is because it was not celebrated by a priest.

Where the unbaptized party gets baptized before the wedding, the impediment of *disparity* is removed and there is no need for a dispensation. But if it is proved afterwards that there was no intention of receiving the sacrament, that the unbaptized one went through the ceremony merely to induce the Catholic to marry him, then he is *not* baptized and the marriage is null.

The next impediment, though it does not arise from any principle peculiar to Catholicism, belongs to Church law only. Therefore it does not affect the unbaptized.

(vi) Crimen

The name is left in Latin as any English translation would be misleading. (The Latin word is misleading, too, as we have noted, but being in Latin is likely to mislead fewer readers.) The impediment arises when the adultery of one party to a marriage is accompanied by a threat to the life of the other. Thus if A and B are married, and A commits adultery with C, and either promises to marry C, or goes through a form of marriage with C, or if either of them kills B—then any subsequent marriage between A and C is null.

Further if, even without adultery, A unites with C in a plot to kill B, a marriage between A and C would be null. The point of the law is to protect the unwanted B. A married man's adultery may be in itself no more than a yielding to temptation involving infidelity to his wife but no actual danger to her; but when it is accompanied by a promise of marriage, he clearly has in contemplation the death of his wife; and an adulterer should not be encouraged to contemplate the death of his wife. If it can be shown that the promise of marriage was dependent not on the death of the unwanted wife but on the possibility of her divorcing A, the impediment would not arise. (There is a faint—but only a faint—suggestion of this in the rule of English law that if X, during his marriage with Y, promises to marry Z, and then, upon Y's death, refuses to carry out his promise, Z cannot succeed against him in an action for breach of promise. The law holds such a promise void, as against public policy.[7])

Extremely complicated questions can arise—thus, if a man kills his wife, not in order to be free to marry his partner in adultery, but because of his rage at discovering that his wife had been guilty of adultery too, no ecclesiastical impediment would arise from the killing (though the civil law might interfere with his marital plans by executing or imprisoning him). No more is attempted here than to give the general notion of the impediment.

The last impediment on our list might seem to belong logically in the next chapter, which considers the necessity and the conditions of free consent. But Canon Law includes it with the impediments.

(vii) *Abduction*

The technical term is *Raptus*. It is laid down by the Council of Trent that if a man carries off a woman with intent to marry her, he cannot do so—even if she says she is willing—as long as she remains in his power. To incur impediment, the man need not actually remove the woman from her own residence: it is sufficient if he has her in his power.

A case in point is given in the *Acta Apostolicae Sedis* (1918, p. 207):

[7] See Wilson v. Carnley, [1908] 1 K.B. 729.

Iang-k'eou-tze, a Catholic, lived in Manchuria with her cousin Kao, by whom she had a son; ten men, including Francis Wang-i-chan (also a Catholic), carried her off to the house of Wang's family and tried to persuade her to marry him; she escaped back to Kao. Five or six armed men brought her back. She said she was willing to marry Wang. Four catechists questioned her on the day before the marriage, and she said she had no cause not to marry him. Four or five armed men guarded her that night and during the wedding there were armed guards at the church door. It was held that her application for nullity must be granted, because whether she was willing or not, this was certainly a case of *raptus*.

The law does not say what would happen if the woman abducted the man; nor does any man appear to have sought a decree of nullity on this ground.

VI

The Parties Did Not Consent

PRACTICALLY all the grounds under this heading may be found in English and American law as well as in the law of the Church. The phrase used by the Canon lawyers, *consensus non concubitus facit matrimonium*—consent, not intercourse, makes a marriage—would be used by the lawyers of England and New York. Nothing whatever is of any use as a substitute for consent. No one can be married without his consent; and consent is an act of the will, not simply words in the mouth. If either party does not consent, the ceremony, however splendid, is a mere form, accomplishing nothing.

Marriage is grounded upon a contract between a man and a woman; unless they agree to marry each other there is no marriage. So far all is simple—no consent, no marriage. But cases arise where there is an appearance of consent yet no genuine consent. They may arise in one of two ways:

   (a) from want of knowledge;
   (b) from some cause affecting the will.

63

A. WANT OF CONSENT FROM
WANT OF KNOWLEDGE

There will be no agreement to marry if one of the parties is insane, or does not know what marriage is, or that he is agreeing to marry, or who it is that he is supposed to be marrying.

(*i*) *Insanity*

Insanity is not listed among the impediments in Canon Law, but by natural law it obviously is one; the Church agrees with England and New York that an insane man is as incapable of making the contract of marriage as of making any other contract. Differences among the three codes relate to the degrees of mental derangement— lunacy, idiocy, mental defect, and so on—and the possibility of lucid intervals. But, in all, the question to be settled is whether in this particular case this particular person knew what he was doing and could be held responsible for it.

The insanity, of course, should have existed at the time of the marriage. But cases in the Rota are decided on the principle that when it exists before and after, it may reasonably be presumed to have existed at the time; and even if there were no actual symptoms of insanity till after, expert evidence may be able to show that a particular form of insanity must have existed before. New York allows an annulment even when the insanity occurs after the marriage provided it has lasted five years.

Church law allows for valid marriage during lucid intervals, so does New York Law; in English Law a lunatic, who has been officially declared so or whose estate is managed by trustees under the Lunacy Laws, cannot marry even during a lucid interval—unless he has meanwhile been officially declared to have recovered his sanity. Since the Matrimonial Causes Act of 1950, a marriage is voidable if one of the parties was, unknown to the other, subject to recurrent fits of insanity. It has been held sufficient for nullity if one of the parties, not insane otherwise, had such delusions on the subject of marriage that "there was not a real appreciation of the engagement apparently entered into".[1] But in practice the probabilities are that the courts of all three codes would give very much the same decisions. Certainly Church courts are fully aware how unlucid lucid intervals may be.

(ii) Ignorance of What Marriage Is

The parties need not know all the physical details of marriage beforehand, but they must at least know that it is for the procreation of children, that this is a process in which both must take part, and that each is giving a right to the other exclusive of all other people.

A case in point is that of Tsi-Tcheng-Lin.[2]

[1] Forster v. Forster (1923) 39 TLR 658; see also Park v. Park (1954), P. 89, 112, C.A.
[2] *Acta Apostolicae Sedis*, 1921, p. 54.

His father bought him a wife, one Maria Hin, aged thirteen. Though he was thirty, he did not know what the ceremony was all about. He could not do the simplest things of daily life; his intelligence was less than that of a boy of seven. Five years later she became a Christian. Later still she took a lover, by whom she became the mother of several sons. Tsi-Tcheng-Lin not only did not complain, but saw nothing odd about it, welcomed the lover *as* lover to the house, did not know enough of the meaning of marriage to realize that his own rights were being infringed. Finally he left her and she sought and was granted a decree of nullity on the ground of *his* want of consent. It was held that for the contract of marriage, the mere use of reason was not sufficient, but a degree of discretion proportioned to the contract—that is, one must know, at any rate vaguely, the nature and essential properties of marriage.

With this case may be compared the English case of *Harrod v. Harrod.*[3]

This was the case of a deaf and dumb woman. But apart from this defect, it was shown that her intelligence was well developed (incomparably more, in fact, than Tsi-Tcheng-Lin's). The marriage was, therefore, held valid, but the test was applied: did the parties sufficiently understand the nature of the contract—that is, did they understand

[3] (1854) 1 K. & J. 4.

that they had agreed to cohabit together during their joint lives, and not to cohabit with any other person?

(iii) *Ignorance of What the Ceremony Was*

In the light of all that has been said, it may scarcely be necessary to mention that if a person went through a ceremony of marriage not knowing what he was doing, then no marriage could result. This might happen either through mistake as to the nature of the ceremony—e.g., thinking it a ceremony of betrothal; or through some more general confusion—e.g., from drunkenness or somnambulism. In *Mehta v. Mehta*,[4] the woman was granted a decree because she had not known she was being married. She thought the ceremony, which was in Hindustani, was only one of conversion to the Hindu religion.

(iv) *Error as to the Person*

If one person goes through the form of marriage with another, thinking that other to be some third person, the marriage is null. Mere error as to the quality of the person one is agreeing to marry—the character, for example, wealth, or social standing—does not make the marriage null. The single exception in Canon Law is that if one married a slave, not knowing that he was one, it would be no marriage. Obviously, a slave, owned by, and at the disposal of, a third person, could not fulfil the obligations

---

[4] 174 L. T. 69.

of married life, might indeed be sold to a new owner in a distant place. Indeed most countries held that a slave could not make any contract.

Until recently English law had no exception at all to the rule that only error as to who the person is makes a marriage voidable; but two exceptions were introduced by the Matrimonial Causes Act of 1937, re-enacted in the Act of 1950. A marriage is now voidable if

(a) one person was subject to recurrent fits of insanity or epilepsy, or was suffering from venereal disease in a form which would render it communicable to the other; or (b) the woman was pregnant by some other man. In both cases, the marriage is voidable only if the condition was unknown to the one now petitioning for nullity.

Observe that both Church law and (with these two exceptions) English law proceed on the principle that all that is required is that this man and this woman freely consent to marry each other. The mere fact that one of them might not have consented if he had known certain things about the other—his or her temper, for instance, or sexual habits, or solvency—has no bearing on the question. And given the importance for society of a stable institution of marriage this is reasonable.

But there is one element of the general law of contract which New York applies to the contract of marriage and the Church and England do not: if one party is, *by the fraud of the other*, led to believe something without which he or she would not have agreed to marry, then the marriage may be declared null upon the petition of the deceived party (the deceiver is bound by it unless the other takes action). The fraud may lie in assertion of what is false or concealment of information that the other party is entitled to have. The author of one textbook[5] quotes a dictum to the effect that it is "as easy to get an annulment in New York as a divorce anywhere in the United States" and goes on to express his own view that "there are more general and particular grounds, both in number and variety, for marriage annulment in New York than for marriage termination in all other States combined". He has counted 150 grounds under the heading of Fraud or Misrepresentation on which marriages have been annulled.

It has been suggested that the reason why New York courts declare marriages void for fraud more easily than other States is that divorce is so much harder to obtain in New York (adultery is the only ground): annulment for fraud is a way out. Certainly other States require that the misrepresentation or concealment should concern one of the essentials of the marriage relation, whereas New York courts (generally anyhow) require only that it should concern some fact or intention, the knowledge of which would have prevented a reasonably prudent person from going on with the marriage.

Thus the courts of other States have refused to annul a marriage where a Catholic was induced to consent by a lying statement that the other party's previous spouse,

[5] Clevenger, *Annulment of Marriage*, p. 29.

divorced and still alive, was dead: this was held not to concern an essential of the marriage relation. It is hard to see a New York court making such a refusal. Civil marriages have been annulled in New York because one party promised that a religious ceremony would follow and refused to keep the promise—on the ground that the promise was made in bad faith, with no intent of keeping it, solely to get the other to consent (and there is a curious case[6] where a marriage was annulled because the man induced the woman to consent to a civil marriage by a promise, not kept, that he would later become a Catholic—she must have been an oddly instructed Catholic herself).

In New York it now seems established as sufficient that the fraudulent pretence must concern a really material fact (in one case a pretence to hold a college degree was held not material enough!). The plaintiff must satisfy the court that, but for the deception, he or she would not have married; and the fraud must not be the sort of a lie that a sensible person would have discounted.

But it is not possible to define these rules with mathematical accuracy.

Courts will differ, judges in the same court will differ. In *Longten v. Longten*[7] it was stated that "misrepresentations must be of existing material facts bearing directly upon the health and happiness of the one who was mis-

6 T. v T. 197 AD 489, 189 NYS 860.
7 1940 Misc 22 NYS 2d 827.

led". A year earlier it had been said in *Williams v. Williams* that the grounds "need not concern the essentials of the marriage relationship; any fraud is adequate but for which the party deceived would not have consented". There seems to be a difference at least of emphasis here. One of the difficulties in the way of the writer on this subject is that only a tiny proportion of the cases in which marriages are declared null are the subject of detailed report. Those I have read have left me with an impression that the Court of Appeals takes a wider view of the fraud that invalidates a contract of marriage than some of the lower courts, tending to lessen or eliminate the distinction between the contract of marriage and contracts generally.

The number of marriages declared null in New York, largely because fraud in inducing consent is a ground for nullity, will strike a Catholic as astronomical. In the five years 1942 to 1946, there were 11,128 decrees of nullity[8] in New York *City* alone. And the proportion of the marriages terminated by annulment to those terminated by divorce is larger than in other States—nearly 28% over the five year period, and rising (it was 18% in 1942 and 35% in 1946). These were war years of course. I have been unable to get comparable figures for more recent years. But in the one year 1950, according to the N.A. Abstract of Statistical Information, there were 11,700 marriages terminated in New York State, and

[8] *Columbia Law Review* (XLVIII), p. 904, footnote.

lawyers tell me that the proportion of annulments to divorces is still very high.

Frequently marriages declared null on the ground of fraud in New York might have been declared so by an English court or a Church court on one of the other grounds. But there is a real difference of principle all the same. For Canon Law and the law of England, apart from the handful of exceptions already stated, free consent makes a marriage, no matter how that consent has been induced.

B. WANT OF CONSENT FROM CAUSES AFFECTING THE WILL

For marriage, we have noted, a man and a woman must *consent* to marry each other. The defects of knowledge we have been discussing directly affect the last four words "to marry each other"—one of the parties not knowing what marriage is, or what the ceremony is, or who the other person is, or, in the case of insanity, what any of it means.

The causes in the will directly affect the consent itself: one of the parties, though uttering consenting words, does not *in fact* consent. The consent is uttered either under compulsion (*force and fear*), or with reservations attached (*condition*), or to gain some other end while excluding marriage (*simulation*).

(i) Force and Fear

There are probably more suits for nullity under this head in Church Law and English Law than under any other (in New York the commonest ground, as we have seen, is fraud). The general principles are common to all three bodies of law. Consent is not free—better, it is not consent—if induced by pressures or threats. For the resultant fear to be a ground of nullity it must be (1) caused by someone else: in 1927 the Rota gave a decree of nullity to a man who had been led to the altar at the point of a gun; but a man who, having seduced a girl, married her through fear of going to Hell if he did not, cannot plead this fear, over-mastering as it may have been, as a ground for nullity; (2) directed to extorting matrimonial consent: if a criminal marries a girl because as his wife she cannot give evidence which might hang him, he cannot use his fear that the public prosecutor would call her as a witness against him as a ground for nullity.

Indeed he would fail in such a plea on another ground as well—the fear must be produced by unjust means, it must be fear of action which the other person is not justly entitled to carry out.

Yet there can be some subtle problems here. In a case decided by the Rota (13 August, 1924), a girl married a man because a rich grandmother had threatened to withdraw all support if she did not. A decree of nullity was given because, though the grandmother was entitled to withdraw her support, she was not entitled to use the threat of its withdrawal to force consent to a marriage.

There is a rather difficult line also to be drawn in those American States where the law entitles a judge to give the man the choice of marrying the girl or going to prison. If the man married the girl, his consent would have been induced by a threat—but would it have been an unjust threat? It is not unjust to attach a prison sentence to seduction; it is not unjust to suspend the sentence if the seducer marries the victim. But it is not easy to draw a line between a man's knowing that marrying a girl will probably save him from prison, and a judge's threatening him with prison if he does not marry her: though of course if the man were wrongly arrested, there would be no problem: the threats would nullify the marriage.

Injustice is usually easy enough to see. Thus the Rota gave a decision for nullity in a case where the man had threatened to tell the girl's parents that she had had intercourse with him, and in another where the girl had threatened to commit suicide if the man did not marry her. That threat alone would not have sufficed, for it was a threat to kill herself not him, but it would have exposed the man to infamy, and she had a rather dangerous brother. A New York court held a marriage null where the man had threatened to kidnap the girl and blow up her parents' house.[9]

A decision given by the Rota (10 May, 1918) is most instructive.[10]

[9] Fratello v. Fratello, 118 Misc 584, 193 NY Supp 865.
[10] *Acta Apostolicae Sedis*, pp. 11–89.

A native South African girl, captured in a war, uttered some kind of matrimonial consent before a priest, though neither she nor the man was baptized. Later both were baptized, lived together for seven years, had nine children. She never ceased to protest against the marriage, but had no means of escaping. A daily communicant, she finally renewed her consent under threat of refusal of the sacraments if she did not. At first opportunity she escaped. The suit was brought by the man, and a decree of nullity given on the ground that the woman had acted through grave fear.

There is a special mode of fear—reverential fear—arising from the respect due to someone (for example, a parent) to whom one is subject, but with some such added reason as ceaseless beseechings, threats, harsh words, and so on.

There is a full discussion of force and fear in general and of reverential fear in the case of Marguerite Guenard and Joseph Iavelle.[11]

The girl, aged nineteen, did not want to marry the man; witnesses deposed that she had shown her dislike very strongly, and begged her mother not to force her to marry him. The mother, not by argument only, but by threats of driving her from the house and even hitting her, had her way. Seventeen years later the couple (who had been consistently

[11] *Acta Apostolicae Sedis*, 1918, p. 70.

inharmonious) separated. She applied for nullity. The court took these facts into account: (1) that the mother admitted the pressure she had exerted (the confession of those who caused the fear being preferable to all other testimony); (2) that the mother was of a domineering character (her husband suffered from this as well as her daughter); (3) that the daughter was weak, yielding, naturally obedient (it is important to note that the question always is—not: "Was the pressure enough to influence the *average* person?", but "Was it too much for the individual concerned?").

As to the length of time—seventeen years—that was sufficiently explained by the fact that she, in common with most other people, knew nothing of the law of nullity.

Another case of this sort is given in the *Acta Apostolicae Sedis.*[12]

Eugénie Le Fortier married Jean-Baptiste Topuzian in 1910. She was nineteen. After three years they separated and obtained a civil divorce. In 1917 she petitioned for a decree of nullity on the ground of force and fear. It was shown that her father forced her (1) with threats of not allowing her to go on living in his house; (2) with threats of refusing to keep her mother—he was anxious to be rid of her that he might be free to look after his illegitimate children and their mother. She had

12 1920, p. 373.

shown signs of sadness on her wedding-day. The
father admitted the threats and added that she
would never have dared to refuse his orders. The
petition was granted.

These cases more or less set out the Catholic doctrine
on the subject. By way of underlining certain points, it
is worth while noting the case of Virginia Marchese.[13]
Here the Rota laid down:

(a) That a trifling degree of fear is no ground for
nullity—if, for example, this girl had not been subject to threats, but only to arguments.

(b) That consent is sufficient for validity: mere
absence of love does not invalidate a marriage; it is
nowhere laid down that marriage must be strongly
desired.

Most of us, I imagine, feel a difficulty about marriages
in countries where the girl's parents invariably choose
the husband—in some, she does not even see him before
the wedding. How is her consent free? If this way of
arranging marriages is so invariable in her world and of
such long standing, it probably never occurs to her that
any other is possible. She may hope (for the most part,
one imagines, not unreasonably) that her parents will
make a pleasing choice; she may have met the man and
disliked him; but either way she does not dream of with-
holding her consent. But if a girl born in such a society

13 *Acta Apostolicae Sedis*, 1918, p. 108.

did learn of other possibilities and decided that she simply would not have the man of her parents' choice but was forced to all the same, the marriage would be null, and would be so declared by a Church court if she could bring suit. Short of universal custom, of course, there have been in all societies, including Catholic societies, tyrannous parents forcing marriages which a Church court would have declared null—but the victim either did not know of the law of nullity or had not the nerve to invoke it.

A careful statement of the law on force and fear will be found in Appendix A, where the *Marlborough Case* is set out in full. For a degree of fear less grave than in the *Marlborough Case* but ground for a nullity decree just the same, see the *Garraud-Pic Case*.[14]

With these Roman cases we may compare certain English cases. In *Scott v. Sebright*,[15] it was laid down that the validity of a contract of marriage must be tested like the validity of any other contract.[16] In order to have a contract held null and void through fear, it is not necessary that the fear should be such that a person of ordinary courage and resolution would yield to it; if the party in question is incompetent to resist pressure improperly brought to bear, then there is not true consent, and consequently no contract.

[14] *Acta Apostolicae Sedis*, 1916, pp. 9–144.
[15] 12 P.D. 21.
[16] This rule must not be taken too literally; there are exceptions to it—for example concerning the effect or non-effect of fraud.

The facts were as follows:

> Miss Scott, an heiress, was induced by Sebright, to whom she was engaged, to accept bills to the amount of twenty and thirty thousand pounds. The discounters threatened her with bankruptcy proceedings and Sebright persuaded her that her only hope of avoiding ruin was to marry him. Just before the ceremony, which took place at a registry office, he threatened to shoot her if she showed she was not acting of her own free will. After the ceremony the parties separated and the marriage was never consummated. Nullity was granted for the reasons given above.

It will be observed that the *principles* on which this case was decided would be sufficient to cover the decisions given in the Roman cases I have quoted; but the *facts* show greater pressure than either. It is a question, therefore, for whoever would compare the two systems, whether an English court would consider facts similar to those in the Roman cases sufficient to secure nullity. I do not bring the New York courts into the comparison, because I have not studied so many of their decisions. Summarizing the Rota cases and the English cases I have been able to examine, the following statements appear to be correct:

> (a) The English cases in which nullity was actually granted all show a greater degree of pressure

than the *least* that has been available to secure a decree of nullity in the Roman courts.

(b) In the English cases where nullity has been refused, it would seem (though this is, of course, no more than my own quite inexpert opinion) that it would equally have been refused by the Roman courts.

(c) Thus the least degree of pressure accepted by Roman courts lies midway between those refused by English courts and those considered sufficient. Nothing quite equivalent appears to have come before the English courts.

The case of *Clarke v. Stier*[17] might easily have come to our assistance but for a complication. In this case the girl was induced by her mother to go through the ceremony of marriage. It was shown that her mother had exercised an abnormal amount of control over the girl; and the courts gave a decree of nullity; but it does not appear whether this ground would have been sufficient if it had not also been shown that the girl thought she was merely going through a ceremony of betrothal.

(d) The *principle* laid down in English cases would, if logically applied, cover *any* nullity decree granted under this head by Roman courts.

At any rate the rule is clear enough in all three codes: no one must be forced to marry; a degree of pressure which makes the consent no longer free invalidates the

[17] [1896], P. 1.

marriage. Both Church and State have two guiding principles: that marriage should be free; and that the stability of society demands that unions should not be lightly upset. It might not be too broad a generalization to say that if there is any difference between the two codes it arises because the Church is more anxious about the first and the State—England anyhow—about the second (though *this* anxiety is less obvious in the matter of divorce!). At any rate a rough working-rule for nullity in Church law is to ask the question: "Did A through fear contract a marriage which but for that fear A would certainly not have contracted?"

Thus not only is it true that no one must be forced to marry; the fact is that no one *can* be forced to marry; the force nullifies the consent without which there can be no marriage. And all who attach any value to the liberty of the individual should be glad that in these three great systems of law it is so carefully secured in a relation of such importance.

(*ii*) Condition

A marriage may be invalidated by a condition made by one of the parties that he agrees to marry only on the understanding that some particular thing (*extrinsic to the marriage contract or relation*) has not happened or will not happen.

The effect of such a condition, if it refers to the present or past, is that if it is fulfilled the marriage comes into being; if it is not the marriage is null. If it refers to the future, then the marriage does not come into being till it is fulfilled.

To affect a marriage the condition must be explicitly attached to the consent in such a way that it clearly makes the consent *provisional*. It is not sufficient that it should be a contract made at the same time, or an agreement without which the matrimonial consent would not have been given. Thus if a party says (implicitly or explicitly), "I do consent *because,* e.g., you have made certain statements or promises," then the statements or promises give rise to the consent but do not in any way *limit* it. If they are false statements, or promises never kept, the consent has been given through error; but still it has been given. But if the party says, "I do consent *provided that*, e.g., such and such a thing is true," then he has only consented provisionally; a condition made in that form means that he has not consented—unless the condition happens to be true.

A case of this sort, where nullity was sought on the ground of a condition relating to the past which was not fulfilled, is the case of B. C. and P. D. in the *Acta Apostolicae Sedis*.[18]

Here the woman agreed to marry the man on the explicit condition that he had never had a mistress. She left him the following year on the discovery that he *had* had a mistress and sought a decree of nullity. This was granted after a long argument, on

[18] 1918, p. 388.

the ground that while a *mistaken view* held by her
as to his past career would not invalidate the marriage (even if she would not have married but for
that view), an *actual condition* certainly did.

In another case the Rota decided for nullity[19] (10
December, 1927) where a girl had married the man on
the explicit condition that he was a rich man, and in fact
he hadn't a penny.

The Church naturally objects strongly to the attach-
ing of conditions to matrimonial consent, save in very
special circumstances; but if the parties make them, and
the Church is not told, she is quite powerless to do anything about it. If the contract *is* made by the parties to
depend on a condition, it simply does; the agreement is
theirs and no one else's.

The distinction between consent given *because of*
statements or promises and consent given *conditionally*
exists equally in English law. *Moss v. Moss*[20] was the case
of a man whose wife proved to have been pregnant at the
time of her marriage to him. (Since 1937 the pregnancy
would be a statutory ground for nullity, but it was not
then.) His petition for nullity was refused for the reason
that *in the case of the contract of marriage* it is sufficient
that the consent be freely given; the contract is not null
because the consent was given in error, or even through
fraud. So far English law agreed with the Church. Would

[19] R.D. 19–517.
[20] [1897] P. 263.

it agree equally that a marriage is null if the consent is made to depend upon a condition which is not fulfilled? Apparently the case has never come before an English court; but the judge in *Moss v. Moss* expressed his belief that the Church view was "the correct view of English law".

It would seem that in New York conditions, attached to the agreement to marry and not complied with, do not directly render the agreement void but can often be brought under the heading of fraud. A most interesting case is *Mirizio v. Mirizio*.[21] There had been a civil marriage, the woman consenting to this only on the man's promise of a Catholic ceremony to follow. She refused to cohabit unless the ceremony took place: he refused the ceremony: she sued for maintenance but did not get it. The Court, by majority, held that her refusal to have ordinary marriage relations disqualified her from claiming support. However good her reason for refusal might seem to her, in the eyes of the Court she was legally married. Had she applied for annulment on the ground that she had been induced by fraud to consent, she might have got it: but by applying for maintenance she asserted the validity of the marriage. In the eyes of the Church, as the next chapter will make clear, she was not married.

(iii) *Simulated Consent*

There is another form of defect of consent, where one of the parties goes through the form of marriage, with

21 242 NY 74, 150 NE 605, 44 ALR 74.

no intention whatever of getting married but simply to attain some object of his own which cannot be obtained otherwise.

The contract of marriage, because of its special importance to the individual and to society, differs in certain ways from other contracts. One is that in other contracts the law will sometimes presume that a man *has* done what he *ought* to have done. If he has so acted that the other party is entitled to expect his signature to an agreement, for example, the law may take his signature as written, even if it is not. This rule is not applied to marriage. In a letter of July 11, 1789,[22] Pope Pius VI says, "In a civil contract the absence of consent may, for certain reasons, be supplied by the law, but no human power can do this in the case of marriage."

Thus if one of the parties gives a fictitious external consent, then the marriage is invalid.

The Rota gave nullity in a case where the man wanted to have sexual relations with the woman for a while, and could not have them without pretending to marry her; and in another case where the man and woman went through the form of marriage solely in order to give a name to their child, and separated after the ceremony. (We have already considered cases where New York has had to decide upon marriages entered into only with the intention of "saving the woman's name", "protecting the child".) A New York court gave nullity where the

[22] Quoted in Smet, *Betrothment and Marriage*.

man married the woman only to get funds for his education and never meant to live with her.

In an English case[23] nullity was decreed where a Hungarian woman had married a foreigner as the one way of getting out of Hungary. There have been several New York cases where foreigners married Americans solely to get into America. They are usually declared null, but in one case nullity was refused because intercourse had taken place with full knowledge on the American's part of what was in the other's mind.

(The situation mentioned above about marrying only to make the child legitimate, but with one new element, gave rise to an interesting decision by a New York court. In the case of *Erickson v. Erickson*,[24] the parties agreed to marry for the same purpose on the same terms; the woman applied for nullity on the ground that the man had violated the condition about no intercourse: the court refused her plea, holding that the condition was against public policy.)

In the nature of things this sort of case is rare—there are not so many things that cannot be obtained without a pretense of marriage—and where it does happen it is usually hard to prove. In the ten years before the publication of the first edition of this work (1920–1930), for instance, only eleven cases on this ground came before the Rota: of these only three were successful (and in one of these cases there were two other grounds). Of course,

[23] H. v. H. 1954 P. 263.
[24] 48 NY Supp 2d 588.

if a ceremony of marriage were gone through obviously as a piece of play-acting or pure fooling, it would not be valid.

At the risk of wearying readers it seems worth while to reiterate what is the very key of the institution of marriage: that the parties, by their consent, make it themselves. After the decree of nullity given in the *Marlborough Case,* it was reported in the papers—falsely, for all I know—that the American Episcopal bishop who officiated at the original ceremony in New York regarded the decision as an insult to himself. To hold such a view is completely to misunderstand the nature of the marriage contract. To criticize a piece of furniture is to criticize the carpenter who made it. But the officiating cleric does not make the marriage; the parties make it. The *Marlborough Case* would equally have resulted in a decree of nullity if the Pope himself had been the celebrant—and indeed most of the nullity decrees granted by the Church are in respect of weddings solemnized by Catholic priests.

The consent of the parties will not make a marriage unless certain other conditions rightly imposed by the rightful authorities have been satisfied; but there can be no marriage without their consent.

VII

Form

BOTH State and Church insist on certain forms being observed: in both, there are some forms whose absence is illegal, but not fatal to the marriage, and some whose absence is fatal.

A. FORM REQUIRED BY THE CHURCH

(i) *The Priest as Witness*

In the Catholic Church, the form is clearly laid down. Since the Council of Trent so decided in 1563, a Catholic must be married before the parish priest (or his delegate) and two other witnesses; otherwise the marriage is clandestine, and therefore null. It must be remembered that the priest is only a *witness;* he does not "make" the marriage. He does not confer the sacrament; the parties confer the sacrament on each other. Therefore the only two people strictly *necessary* to the celebration are the man and woman concerned. Until 1563 no formalities were required, only the consent of the parties. Some sort of religious ceremony was usually required to make the marriage licit, but for validity it was enough that the man and woman should make clear that they were now taking, or had taken, each other as husband and wife. This, called in England common law marriage, was not forbidden by English law till 1753. It has been invalid in New York since 1933.

In a relationship of this sort, it is obvious that secrecy or semi-secrecy could give rise to problems. The Church now insists on the presence of witnesses—one of whom must be the bishop of the diocese, or else the parish priest or some priest delegated by him.

The chapter *Tametsi* of the Decrees of the Council of Trent, which set this out as the form required in the future, was not promulgated in Protestant countries, including England, so that Catholics could still contract marriages in these countries, valid in the eyes of the Church, by consent. This gave rise to an interchange of letters between Napoleon and Pope Pius VII. In 1803 Napoleon's brother Jerome, aged nineteen, had married Eliza Patterson in Baltimore. The Bonaparte family made a double effort to get a decree of nullity. Jerome's mother protested against the marriage, claiming that her son, being under twenty-one, could not validly marry without her consent: but the Church does not require the consent of parents. Napoleon asked the Pope to annul the marriage, one of the grounds he urged being that the parish priest was not at the wedding: the Pope replied that the decree *Tametsi* had not been promulgated in

Baltimore, and that it was beyond his power to dissolve a marriage that was certainly valid. (The episcopal court of Paris made no such difficulty!)

But from 1908 the *Ne Temere* decree, whose rules are nearly, though not quite, identical with those of *Tametsi*, removed this exemption from English-speaking countries and most others. The few exceptions have since been abrogated, so that the requirement of marriage before the parish priest and two witnesses now extends to *all* Catholics of the Latin rite (save where it is impossible, as below). Thus it does not apply to the Uniates (except certain Ruthenians). And it does not apply to non-Catholics. It does apply to every marriage in which at least one of the parties is a Catholic.

The priest is only a witness and not one of the principals. If it is not possible to have a priest, and the impossibility is likely to continue for a month, or if there is danger of death, then the marriage may be performed without a priest. Otherwise this form is obligatory on Catholics: any Catholic who tries to marry not observing this rule simply is not married.

In technical language, his union is null because of *clandestinity*. To modern ears it is a curious word to use (English law has it too). A Catholic film star, let us say, marries before a Justice of the Peace. The street is blocked with sightseers, every newspaper in the country has its reporters there, the newsreel cameras do their busy work. In due course the actor applies for and gets a decree of nullity from the Church on the ground of clandestinity—secrecy, hiddenness. The meaning, of course, is that the ceremony was not observed by the one witness required for a Catholic marriage, the priest; it was hidden from the face of the Church.

The most famous case on clandestinity is the so-called divorce of Napoleon (as we have seen, he had already tried to get a nullity decree on this ground for his brother).

Napoleon married Josephine in 1796 by a purely civil ceremony. This union was certainly defective in form—clandestine. It was therefore no more a marriage in the sight of the Church than the union of two Catholics before a priest without the presence of a registrar would be a marriage according to the law of England. Fearing that Napoleon would have the marriage annulled, Josephine informed Pope Pius VII, who had come to Paris for the coronation of Napoleon. The Pope refused to crown the Emperor until the marriage was rectified and Cardinal Fesch (who had received from the Pope all the dispensations necessary for the execution of his duties as First Chaplain to the Emperor) married the pair without witnesses in the private apartments at the Tuileries. In 1807 Napoleon, wishing to marry Marie Louise, sought a declaration of nullity from the Diocesan Courts in Paris, on the grounds (1) that he had not freely consented to the second ceremony, but had acted under pressure; (2) that the ceremony had lacked the presence of the parish priest and two witnesses, and that the Papal dispensation had not specifically covered this defect of form. The court of first instance decided in favour of nullity, and on appeal to a second Parisian court this decision was upheld, mainly on the ground of defect of form, though by Napoleon's strong desire want of consent was also given as a ground for the decision. Pius VII protested that the sentence was illegal, on the ground that the Parisian courts were acting outside their jurisdiction (since the marriage of princes belonged to the Pope's jurisdiction directly), but not that it was intrinsically unjust. On this he never gave a ruling—possibly (though this is merely an opinion) because, as Josephine did not appeal against the decree, the case never came before him. Its justice must remain doubtful, since it depends on whether the wording of the dispensations given to Cardinal Fesch by the Pope were technically sufficient to dispense from the necessity of the witnesses demanded by the Council of Trent. The dispensations covered his duties as chaplain to the Emperor, but was the celebration of marriage part of the duties of a chaplain? There is a discussion of this and certain other cases in the *Dictionnaire Apologétique* under the heading "Divorce des Princes".

Since the *Motu Proprio* of Pius XII (1 August 1948) all who have been baptized as Catholics, whether or not they were brought up outside the Church, are bound to be married before the priest and it is no marriage if they are not. In the Latin rite, the witness is usually the pastor of the bride; if the man and the woman belong to different rites—one Latin and one Melchite for example, or one Melchite and one Ruthenian—the general rule is that the pastor of the bride should witness the ceremony.

Although the priest is only a witness, his presence is strictly required. And he must *really* be present—if to secure his bodily presence one of the parties got him so drunk that he did not know what was happening, the marriage would be invalid.

(ii) Marriage without a Priest

There are, as has been mentioned, certain exceptions to the strictness of the requirement that a priest be present. In danger of death, for instance, two witnesses suffice, even without a priest. The same rule applies if the parties could get to the priest (or the priest to the parties) only with serious difficulty: the priest is to be regarded as unobtainable; and if the situation is likely to last for a month, the parties may marry without his presence. But if their belief that the priest is unobtainable happens to be wrong, then their marriage is invalid.

One special form of "unobtainability" is worth mentioning. In countries where (a) the law forbids a Church marriage under heavy penalties unless there has first been a civil marriage, and (b) the civil authorities will not permit a civil marriage—because, e.g., of the absence of documents required by them—then Catholics may be married in the presence of two witnesses, with no priest present.

Apart from such exceptional cases, a Catholic who goes through a civil form of marriage only is not merely committing a most grave sin, but is not married at all. If his wedding is in a non-Catholic church, the marriage is still null and the sin is greater. If, however, the civil law requires marriage before one who is in fact a Protestant minister, Catholics do not sin who go through the form of marriage before him, regarding him simply as a State official, and without his performing any religious ceremony.

B. MIXED MARRIAGES

The section of the Church's marriage-law which deals with clandestinity is probably better known and more generally disapproved than all the rest put together, not because of any strong general interest in Catholic ceremonial or disciplinary regulations, but because this is the rule under which the difficult cases of "mixed marriages" arise.

"Mixed marriages" are marriages in which one party is a Catholic, the other a baptized non-Catholic. The Church discourages such marriages: she has seen too often how dangerous, even disastrous, they can be to the man and woman concerned and to the children of the marriage: for one that works out well, far too many work out ill. She consents to them reluctantly, and grants a dispensation only for good reasons and provided that the non-Catholic party agrees (i) that any children of the marriage shall be brought up as Catholics; and (ii) that the faith of the Catholic party shall not be endangered; and the Catholic party must promise to do his best to convert the non-Catholic. If the dispensation is granted, then the parties may be married in the presence of a priest, as the rule demands. If the dispensation is not granted—and equally, of course, if it is not sought—then the parties cannot be married at all. It occasionally happens that they go through a form of marriage before a registrar or before a clergyman of some non-Catholic church—both of them forms of marriage which the Church would regard as perfectly adequate for the marriage of two non-Catholics. But no marriage results, because one of the parties is a Catholic, and cannot be married save in the form prescribed for Catholics.

It will be noted from this explanation:

(1) that the Church does not make this form binding for non-Catholics. For them she accepts any form regarded as adequate by the authority of the State to which they belong. Thus a registry-office marriage of two non-Catholics is not only regarded by the Church as valid and binding, but, if they are baptized, also as a sacrament;

(2) that the rule has only an accidental connection with "mixed marriages". It is a rule for the marriage of Catholics; and registry-office marriages, for example, are

equally invalid for two Catholics as for a Catholic and a non-Catholic.

Here occurs one more opportunity of stating the principle of principles with regard to the contract of marriage; that, as the parties make the marriage, their consent is essential, and nothing can make up for the lack of it. For a case which constantly arises in argument, however infrequently in real life, is this: A (a Catholic) and B (a non-Catholic) go through the form of marriage at a registry office. They live together as husband and wife for some time and have several children. Then A, who has known all along that the marriage was a nullity, secures a decision to that effect, goes off to a Catholic country, and marries a Catholic girl in a Catholic church. A has, of course, acted abominably (towards God in the first place, since his living with B when he knew he was not married to her was a mortal sin; and in the second place towards B), and it is sometimes asked: "Why does not the Church insist on his marrying B, at any rate if she is willing to marry him, and the faith of the children can be safeguarded?" In fact the Church cannot: there can be no marriage where one of the parties does not consent freely; and you cannot force a man to consent freely.

C. FORM REQUIRED BY THE CIVIL AUTHORITY

I have said that this rule is, in principle, in English law and, one imagines, in the law of all civilized countries.

The *principle* is that a society insists on the presence of an official recognized by it if a marriage is to be valid.

The Church insists on the presence of a priest; the State insists on the presence of a registrar or a minister of the Established Church. The 1861 case *Beamish v. Beamish* is charming: a clergyman of the Church of England officiated at his own wedding: the marriage was declared void—the minister whose presence is required by law must not be the bridegroom: the point could not arise in the Catholic Church!

In all states of the United States marriages may be performed either by a civil official, as in England, or by any minister of the Gospel ordained or licensed according to the rules of his denomination, and by leaders of the Society for Ethical Culture in Manhattan and Brooklyn.

Cases of the State's insistence occur in England every day: when Catholics marry in their own Church, the State registrar or his deputy must be present; if he is not, then the State does not recognize the marriage. (Complications, which need not be discussed here, arise when the English marry abroad.)

But it is not only with regard to the necessary official that English law is stringent (as stringent as the Church's). There are all sorts of other points of form which will nullify a marriage in English law, to which the law of the Church has nothing corresponding. It would be endless to go into all the points, but one or two may be quoted.

Thus if any persons knowingly and wilfully intermarry in any place not recognized by the law as a place in which marriages may be celebrated, the marriage is void. Again, the publication of the banns in a false name to the knowledge of both parties renders the marriage void. In *Midgeley v. Wood*,[1] the man's Christian name was wrongly given, to the knowledge of both parties, the woman consenting only because he told her that it would not invalidate the marriage. But it did.

Again there is the case of *Wormald v. Neale*:[2]

In the publication of the banns, the woman's name was given as Morumild. In the vestry before the wedding she told the clergyman, who called out the names from the banns-book in the presence of both, what her name was, and he entered it correctly in the marriage register. The court held that the publication of banns had not been duly made, and pronounced the marriage null and void.

Consider one more case, the case of *Lawford v. Davies*:[3]

The man and girl, domiciled in England, arrived in Scotland about 4 A.M. of July 1st, 1870; they remained there until July 21st, and between 11 and 12 of that day went through a form of marriage before a registrar. The Scotch Marriage Act demands

---

[1] 30 L.J. 57.
[2] 19 L.J. 93.
[3] (1878) 4 P.D. 61.

twenty-one days' residence. As the Scotch method of reckoning time for legal purposes is from midnight to midnight, the court held that they had not lived in Scotland the full time required by statute and that the marriage was invalid.

As I have said, the English insistence on form is, on the whole, greater than the Church's; yet if it sometimes seems exaggerated, one sees that in a contract of such importance to society some regulation is needed, and whenever there are regulations there are border-line cases.

America has one interesting rule in this field. In some States (New York is *not* one of them) if a person who is, and intends to remain, a resident of the State goes to another State to contract a marriage which would have been void in his own, it *is* void in his own—in Mississippi, Virginia, and West Virginia the rule is aimed only, or (it would seem) mainly, at marriages between white people and coloured. (When is a person "coloured" within the meaning of this law? Missouri says he is coloured if he has one-eighth Negro blood.)

A summary of this section on Form shows interesting parallels between English law and Church law. The State holds that a marriage of its subjects is null which is not celebrated before its official; the Church holds that a marriage of *its* subjects is null which is not celebrated before *its* official. So far there is not much in it! But the parallel goes further, for both authorities allow exceptions: the State says that Jews and Quakers may be validly married according to the form laid down by their religion; the Church says that baptized non-Catholics may be validly married according to the form laid down by their State. And neither Church nor State says that marriage is a private matter affecting the parties and no one else, and therefore capable of valid celebration in any way the parties like.

VIII

Effects of a Decree of Nullity

A. ON THE PARTIES

A DECREE of nullity is a statement that the parties were never married. This is so in the law of England and in the law of the Church, and with certain qualifying considerations (see page 26) in the law of New York. An English case is *Newbould v. Attorney General.*[1]

N.'s father was married in 1909 to a woman on account of whose impotency the marriage was annulled in 1929. Before the annulment N. was born of another woman. After the annulment N.'s father married N.'s mother. A claim was made for N. to be declared legitimated by the subsequent marriage of his parents. The Legitimacy Act, s.1 (2), says: "Nothing in this Act shall operate to legitimate a person whose father or mother was married to a third person when the illegitimate person was born." It was held that N. was entitled to his declaration of legitimacy, for though he was born before his father's marriage to a third person was annulled,

[1] 1929, W.N.

yet the annulment was a declaration that the marriage had never existed.

We now come to a point of quite enormous importance. In Church law a decree of nullity is merely a *declaration;* it does not alter the facts. The court decides on the facts presented to it; applying the law to those facts, it gives a decree either for nullity or for validity. But if, either by accident or by the design of the parties, it has not *all* the facts, or if it has falsehood offered to it as truth, then its decision may be erroneous. The decree does not and cannot possibly alter the *fact;* two people either are married to one another or they are not. Nothing that *any* court can say will alter that. Thus, if an erroneous decree of nullity is given, the marriage is still valid. If an erroneous decree of validity is given, the marriage is still null.

What, then, is the point of the decree? Simply this: Whenever there has been the *appearance* of marriage, if one or both of the parties wish to dispute its *reality,* they are not allowed simply to decide their own case. No matter how obvious it may seem that the marriage *is* null, the Church insists that her members shall not be judge in their own case, shall not marry someone else until a decree from the Church has been obtained. This is necessary to avoid scandal, to prevent serious irregularities, and to make quite certain that the new marriage is valid. Even given high doctrinal and legal competence, an interested party may not be the best judge.

The decision once given means that the parties are now free in conscience to marry a third person—provided that they do not know of some fact not placed before the court which would have affected the decision. Given absolute honesty in the parties, a mistake by the court in declaring for nullity is practically impossible. But if it did occur, and the court gave a decree of nullity mistakenly, the original marriage would still exist; the parties might contract another union—and they would not be in sin (since they had acted honestly throughout) —but the second union would not be a marriage; the first marriage still stands, and, while both parties are alive, neither can marry again.

A decree of a matrimonial court is not infallible, and is never final. It is not *res judicata*—that is, it may always be re-opened *if fresh evidence comes to hand*. It is simply the best opinion that can be offered on the facts put before the court.

It is not possible to say what is the ruling of English law on this point. Is a decree of nullity issued by a competent English court final, so that the matter cannot be re-opened, no matter what evidence may later emerge to show that the decree was given in error? Logically it is not. But the case does not seem to have arisen.[2] A case that is analogous to that of a Catholic who honestly contracts another union after a decree of nullity, is that of a person in England who is legally allowed to presume the

---

[2] This question is not treated in English legal text-books, but *Wilkins v. Wilkins* (1896 P. 108) suggests what the answer might be.

death of a partner of whom nothing has been heard for seven years, and marries again. In the first case, if the decree of nullity was erroneous, then (according to Church law) the parties to the second union are not married—though while they remain ignorant of the error there is no sin. In the second case, if the partner presumed dead happens to be alive, then (according to English law) the parties to the second union are not married, though they are guiltless of the crime of bigamy.

Obviously the Church courts, like any other courts, might be deceived by a perjurer. But from what has just been said, the actual advantage gained by a perjurer is nil. As a Catholic he knows that, if he *is* married, he is, and that a decree of nullity fraudulently obtained would be merely waste paper, leaving his existent marriage where it is, so that any effort to contract a further marriage is fruitless and in addition is a deadly sin. If he is a person of small faith and easy conscience, prepared to commit such a sin, there is ordinarily no reason why he should go to a great deal of trouble fraudulently to get from the Church a piece of waste paper when he could with no trouble at all proceed straight to the commission of a simpler and less complicated, if no less mortal, sin. To go through the form of marriage with a third party while one's present partner is alive is a mortal sin; to perjure oneself in a nullity court and then go through the form of marriage with a third party is two mortal sins.

Still there *are* situations in which a person might be prepared to commit perjury. The one he wishes to marry may have the conscience he lacks, so that she will not marry him unless his first marriage is declared null; or, in a country with a large Catholic population, a plainly adulterous second marriage might damage his career. The Rota (not to mention the Defender of the Bond) is extremely vigilant; no court is proof against the possibility of deception, but a court whose decisions are not final and irrevocable has less cause to fear it than any other.

B. ON THE LEGITIMACY OF THE OFFSPRING

Many people, who see the logic of the Church's teaching on nullity, are troubled by the thought of the children rendered illegitimate by the declaration that their parents were never married. To this both Church and State may very well reply, that however deeply one may sympathize, yet the facts are beyond their control. Illegitimacy is *never* the fault of the children. If parents are not married, they are not. But a void marriage is not the same thing as a liaison, and in all three codes allowance is made for this.

New York goes furthest. In a general way it may be said that the children are legitimate—with an interesting provision unknown to English law or Church law, that they may in certain cases be the legitimate children of one party but not of the other: capable therefore of inheriting from one party and not from the other: in bigamy, for instance, the offspring are the legitimate children of the innocent party (if there is one).

In English law the position now is that upon a declaration of nullity in respect of a voidable marriage, the children are legitimate if they would have been so had the marriage terminated in divorce instead of nullity. The Church, which has always stretched the limits of legitimacy as wide as possible, enacts that the children of a putative marriage are legitimate—a putative marriage is one where there is the appearance of a marriage though in fact no marriage, yet where both parties were free to marry at the time of the contract, and one at least is in good faith.

The Committee for the Authentic Interpretation of the Code declared (26 January 1949) that, for a Catholic, marriage can be putative only if contracted in proper legal form as required for Catholic marriages: thus registry office marriages are not putative. For a Catholic, a ceremony without a priest (if the priest is available) has not even the appearance of a marriage.

Note. It may scarcely be necessary to mention that where a man gets a decree of nullity from the Church and not from the State, then the State regards him as being still married; and if he proceeds to take a wife, the Church will call it marriage, but the State will call it bigamy. While it is true that English courts are coming to regard bigamy more and more leniently—even lightly —it is doubtful if they would extend their leniency to the case of a "bigamist" who in the eyes of his Church was not one.

IX

Dissolution of Marriage

CERTAIN technical terms used by the Church are to be noted. Where both parties are baptized, the term is *matrimonium ratum*. Otherwise it is *matrimonium legitimum*. The only marriage that is *absolutely* indissoluble is the consummated marriage of the baptized—*matrimonium ratum et consummatum*.

Sacramental marriage has a special quality that other marriage has not, in that it symbolizes the unbreakable union of Christ and His Church. And "that symbolism is found fully only in the consummated union".

In the decretal *Ex publico*, the twelfth-century Pope Alexander III states that without consummation, the "final confirmation must needs be wanting" to Our Lord's words on indissolubility. Only by consummation do husband and wife become one flesh; without that their marriage *can* be dissolved, though only by the Church.

It is true that consent makes a marriage; but the marriage it makes, though no human power can dissolve it, is not utterly and in every circumstance indissoluble all the same.

The Church does allow the dissolution of sacramental

marriage, if it has not been consummated; and of non-sacramental marriage, even if consummated, in certain circumstances. And these are cases not of nullity—for the marriage does exist—but of dissolution.

A. NON-CONSUMMATED MARRIAGE

If two baptized persons, or one baptized and one un-baptized, marry and do not consummate the marriage, it may be dissolved in one of two ways:

(1) By the solemn profession of one of the parties in a Religious Order. For entry into the novitiate, there would have to be a dispensation from Rome, and it would not ordinarily be granted unless the other party agreed.

(2) By a Papal dispensation. This may be granted, if the Pope sees fit, even if one of the parties objects. Just cause must be shown—deliberate desertion immediately after the ceremony by one of the parties, for example; danger (which might perhaps have been realized sooner) to faith or morals; the extreme unlikelihood of the parties ever establishing a proper life together. Once the dispensation is granted, the petitioner is free to marry.

Probably the most famous case under this heading is the dissolution by Pope Alexander VI of Lucrezia Borgia's marriage to Giovanni Sforza.[1] She swore that the marriage had not been consummated. Sforza at first

[1] Pastor, *History of the Popes*, vol. v, pp. 520–1.

protested that this was untrue, but under pressure from his family he made a declaration in writing that there had been no consummation. If this was true, it constituted a normal ground for dissolution. Alexander VI accepted their statement. The rest of Rome, which believed that Lucrezia was the Pope's daughter, was more sceptical.

B. NON-SACRAMENTAL MARRIAGE

In his Allocution of 3 October 1941, Pope Pius XII said of marriages that are not sacramental:

> "Other marriages, though intrinsically they are indissoluble, have not absolute extrinsic indissolubility—i.e. granted certain prerequisites (and the cases, of course, are rare) they can be dissolved, not only in virtue of the Pauline Privilege, but also by the Roman Pontiff, in virtue of his ministerial power. . . . In all such cases the supreme norm by which the Roman Pontiff uses his power as Christ's vicar to dissolve the bond of marriage is . . . the salvation of souls. . . . Not only the welfare of religious society and human society generally, but of individual souls will receive due and proportionate consideration."

(i) The Pauline Privilege

This is based upon an instruction given by St. Paul, 1 Corinthians vii. 12–15:

"If any of the brethren has a wife, not a believer, who is well content to live with him, there is no reason why he should put her away, nor is there any reason for a woman to part with her husband, not a believer, if he is content to live with her. . . . On the other hand, if the unbeliever is for separating, let them separate; in such a case the brother or the sister is under no compulsion."

If two unbaptized people marry, one of them is later baptized and the other will not live, or will not live peaceably, with the Christian, then the Christian may marry again and the second marriage dissolves the first.

A fundamental principle here seems to be that baptism really makes a new person, and the new person is free to marry again provided the rights of the first partner are not infringed. If the first partner abandons his rights, then there is no bar to remarriage. He may abandon them by refusing to continue life together (or to resume it if the first marriage had already broken up), or again by behaviour which makes life together unbearable, especially for a Christian.

The Church must be satisfied that the unbaptized partner really *has* abandoned his rights. Normally he must be questioned as to his willingness to resume "peaceful cohabitation"—though this may not be held necessary if the facts speak clearly enough. Further, if it is the newly-baptized partner who causes the broken peace—by infidelity for instance, or constant nagging—she is not entitled to the Pauline Privilege. (In these two paragraphs "he" is used for the unbaptized partner and "she" for the baptized; it could, of course, be the other way round.)

(ii) The Good of Souls

The Pauline Privilege applies where both parties are unbaptized at the time of the original marriage. But there are also instances where the Church has terminated a marriage of baptized with unbaptized when the unbaptized party received baptism.

In one case a baptized non-Catholic married a Jewish woman before a magistrate; they were divorced, the woman was baptized and wanted to marry a Catholic; the dispensation was granted.

There have been a number of similar cases, where the dissolution has been allowed *in favorem fidei* or for the good of souls.

The same line has been taken even where a Catholic has married an unbaptized person with a dispensation, the marriage has broken up, and it is the Catholic who wants to marry again.

(iii) Polygamous Marriages

There is space here to mention, but hardly to discuss,[2] certain papal constitutions issued after the discoveries of new worlds in the sixteenth century.

In the brief *Romani Pontificis* (1571) Pius V deals

[2] See Joyce, *Christian Marriage*, pp. 493 ff.

with often-married Indians converted to the Church and permitted to retain, not the first wife but the wife who is baptized with them.

In the brief *Populis ac Nationibus*, Gregory XIII provided that slaves brought across the sea and separated from their wives might after baptism be allowed to marry again, if contact had been lost with their first partners; and these marriages would be valid even if it later proved that the first partners had themselves been baptized before the second marriage.

It has since become the practice in the mission field to let a polygamist, now a Catholic, keep the wife of his choice, if she too becomes a Christian.

There has been a vast amount of discussion of the theological implications of all this. But at least one has the feeling that, whatever the claims of the first wife, she married in the full awareness that she was gaining no exclusive rights over her husband.

APPENDIX A

THE MARLBOROUGH CASE[1]

1. Born of a rich American family, Consuela Vanderbilt, a baptized non-Catholic, at the age of seventeen fell
in love with a certain M— R—, to whom she became
secretly engaged. But her mother, when she learnt of
this, refused to accept her daughter's engagement; and
further, to destroy the love that had sprung up in her
daughter's heart, she took her to Europe (in1894). Since
Consuela was a girl endowed with youth, beauty, and
great fortune, as well as a brilliant education, she planned
to marry her to a man in the highest ranks of the English
nobility. And in London she came upon Charles, Duke of
Marlborough, and invited him as a guest to her home at
Newport in the United States of America, whither
mother and daughter straightway returned.

Charles accepted the invitation, and in September,
1895, went to Newport, where he stayed with the Vanderbilt family some fifteen days. On the day before his
departure, Charles proposed to Consuela herself, who
pleaded with her mother: but with no success: for the

[1] Translated from the report given in the *Acta Apostolicae Sedis*
(1926, p. 501) of the hearing of the Marlborough Case at the Rota,
on appeal by the *defensor vinculi* from the affirmative decision of
the diocesan court of Southwark, England.

114

mother caused the daily papers to publish the news of the engagement. Whence it came about that, after a journey through Canada, the day appointed for the marriage being at hand, the Duke at last returned to Consuela, to whom he was wedded at New York on the 6th of November, 1895, in a Protestant Church, since he also was a non-Catholic.

The marriage began badly; for soon after, the wife told her husband that she had gone to the altar unwillingly and forced by her mother, and that she was deeply in love with the other man. As their minds were thus discordant, and as the Duke seriously neglected his wife, in 1905, there being now two children, they ceased to live together. In 1920, by mutual consent, they obtained a civil divorce, and each remarried. Finally in 1925 the woman began an action for nullity of her marriage with the Duke in the Matrimonial Court of Southwark, which on the 9th of February, 1926, after due trial gave sentence of nullity of marriage on the ground of *vis et metus*. The *defensor vinculi* appealed to the Holy Office; wherefore the cause now comes to be tried afresh under the usual formula—"Is it agreed as to nullity of marriage in this case?"

2. *As to the law:* The ground is *metus reverentialis*, which certainly by the unvarying opinion of canonists, by the sanction of the Code of Canon Law, and the uniform practice of the Rota, renders a marriage void if, in addition to other conditions, it is grave, and is directed

to the extortion of consent. (Gasparri, *De Matr.* n. 942; Wernz, *Jus. decr.* iv, n. 264; Can. 1087 Cod.; S.R. Rota, *in Parisien.*, 27 julii 1910; *Tarvisina*, 11 mart. 1912; Transylvanien., 1 maii 1912; N.N. *coram Lega.*, 16 maii 1912; *Hyderabaden.*, 2 aug. 1921.)

3. *As to the facts:* The Fathers thought it especially worthy of remark that, when the petitioner had given her promise of marriage to M— R—, whom she passionately loved, her mother had violently resisted the marriage, and exerted all her force to turn her daughter's mind from the man and prevent marriage with him. On this point the petitioner has said: "My mother dragged me away from the influence of my suitor. She took me from my country, intercepted all the letters that he wrote to me and I wrote to him. She made continual scenes. She said that I must obey; that she knew that I had no right to choose a husband; that I must accept the man of her choice; that my opposition was ruining her health, and that I might be the cause of her death. There was a terrible scene when she told me that if I succeeded in escaping, she would seize the first opportunity to shoot my lover, that she would then be put in prison and hanged, and that I should be responsible." This account is confirmed not only by the mother, but also by witnesses, in all its particulars, so that there need be no doubt whatever of its truth.

4. But further it seemed to the Fathers, not only that the mother had forcibly separated her daughter from the man she loved, but in addition that she had forced her to marry the Duke of Marlborough. In this matter, since one who alleges fear should prove it not by proofs of *any* sort, but by such as generate moral certainty of the existence of fear, the petitioner has brought before the Court a great many things which truly prove the fear. She has said: "Having destroyed the possibility of my marriage with the man I loved, my mother told me that she had chosen a man whom she considered suitable in every respect, that he was coming to America to stay with her as a guest, that she had already talked with him of marriage. . . . I persist in my statement that if I consented to marriage with the Duke of Marlborough, it was under the strongest pressure from my mother and according to her absolute will. In addition to the threats which have been mentioned elsewhere, my mother told me many times that if I persisted in opposing her will, it was, given her state of health, a vexation such as might lead to her death. This was also the opinion of the doctor, which was known to me through a friend of my mother, Mrs. Jay, who had it from her." The mother therefore substituted another man for the man she loved, and since she was extremely anxious for a noble title and her daughter was endowed with every womanly grace and immensely rich, as soon as she had met the Duke in London, she invited him straightway to Newport as her guest, that

she might not so much *propose* him to her daughter as a husband, but quite literally *appoint* him: "She said that I must obey, that she knew well that I had no right to choose a husband: I must take the man of her choice."

5. Yet, though the sworn testimony of the one who has suffered fear is held in law as a thing of the greatest weight in proving nullity of marriage on this ground (since the sufferer has experienced the fear and knows it directly, others only by the symptoms)—still it has not the force of proof unless it is properly confirmed by the deposition of other witnesses and by legitimate presumptions. For the Duke has given evidence that about twenty days after the wedding he learnt from his wife that she had contracted the marriage because she had been forced by her mother: "She told me that her mother had insisted upon her marrying me; that her mother was violently opposed to her marriage with M— R—, and that every sort of constraint, pushed even to physical violence, had been employed to attain her end."

Consuela's mother, who caused the fear, has admitted and declared: "I forced my daughter to marry the Duke. I always had an absolute influence over my daughter, my children having been entirely committed to me after my divorce: I had had their education solely in my own hands. When I gave an order, no one argued. Therefore I did not ask her, I commanded her to marry the Duke. . . . I then invited the Duke to visit me at Newport. He came and he stayed about a fortnight. Then I told my daughter that he was the man I had chosen for her. She was completely overcome, and replied that she could not marry him. I considered that I was justified in overriding her opposition as simply the folly of an inexperienced girl."

The aunt of the petitioner gave evidence: "The marriage was imposed by my sister on her daughter who, as I have already said, wanted to marry someone else."

To the Court's inquiry: "Do you consider that the constraint was simple persuasion or really coercion?" Mrs. Lucy Jay affirmed on oath: "Not persuasion at all, but absolute coercion, I swear it, I know it."

Therefore since that proof must be held full and perfect which is made by two unexceptionable witnesses (Reiff., lib. IV, tit. XIX, *de Divortiis*), it is clear that the fear is proven; for the parties and the witnesses are, by the declaration of the Bishop of Southwark, of the Court of Paris and of certain parish priests, thoroughly worthy of belief.

This conclusion is strengthened the more by the aversion Consuela felt for the Duke: "His arrogant character created feelings of hostility in me. He had the air of despising everything not English; my pride was offended." With this declaration, the evidence of her aunt agrees.

6. The Fathers held that there could be no doubt of the gravity of the fear. For fear may be considered grave even when there are no threats or blows; and the indignation of parents is in itself not only an evil, but—if it is

severe and lasting—a grave evil, as the Authors commonly teach, and Clericatus (*De Matrim.,* dec. 37, n. 24) clearly states: "*Metus reverentialis* is considered in two ways according as it is accompanied or not accompanied by danger. In the first way, when the son or daughter, not obeying a father's will . . . reasonably fears to render the father hostile to him, frowning, harsh of aspect, stern of speech and much beside, all these things are felt as grave evils not to be borne,"—so that, if the papers in the present case are examined, the gravity of the fear is conclusively seen. For all the witnesses state that the girl married Charles, overcome by the will of a mother who was not to be resisted, whence the danger of her wrath was very much to be feared by Consuela if the proposed marriage did not take place; especially if it is considered that she trembled in her presence, being a girl gentle, meek and accustomed to obey, and subject to a mother imperious, unused to contradiction, bending all things to her unbridled self-will. . . .

Further, unless she married Charles, a second serious evil and peril was to be feared by Consuela—namely the death of her mother; and this on the opinion of the doctor, with which the mother frequently threatened her daughter, as the petitioner relates in her third interrogation: "In addition to the threats mentioned elsewhere, my mother several times told me that if I persisted in opposing her will, it was, seeing her state of health, a vexation such that it might lead to her death. This was also the opinion of the doctor, which was known to me from a friend of my mother, Mrs. Jay, who learnt it from her." This sworn assertion Mrs. Tiffany, an aunt of the petitioner, confirms: "My sister made continual scenes with her daughter, and tried to win her by telling her she had a weak heart and that if she continued to resist her, she would die."

7. Notwithstanding these things, Consuela did not readily agree to her mother's command. For it is shown that in the first instance the girl gave no assent to the man when he asked her to marry him, but shed tears—and next day read the engagement, which she had assuredly not entered upon, published in the daily papers. Of the quarrels between mother and daughter on account of the daughter's resistance to the marriage, the witnesses sufficiently testify. In short, having no one to whom she might appeal—not to her father, both because under the terms of the divorce by which her father and mother were separated she was under the power of her mother only, and because the father himself had suffered the influence of his wife's indomitable will—as the threats did not cease and the mother's decision remained inflexible, Consuela at last entered into wedlock with Charles. But it is clear that Consuela had been compelled to choose the marriage that she might be freed from fear.

And the mother, fearing that Consuela might at the last moment withdraw the assent which had been extorted from her, on the wedding day placed a guard at her bedroom door, that no one might have access to her or speech with her. And Consuela entered upon marriage with such grief that the Duke has said: "She arrived very late and looked upset."

8. The marriage thus contracted by Consuela under grave fear was not validated by subsequent ratification. For the validation of her consent it would be necessary that the petitioner should have known of the nullity of the marriage through defect of consent, and that she should have renewed matrimonial consent while the married life continued in being. But it is unlikely that Consuela was possessed of canonical knowledge as to the impediments which invalidate marriage, the more so as she belonged to a non-Catholic sect; and, besides, this knowledge is not to be presumed in women but must be proved (cfr. 1.9 pr., D., *De iuris et facti ignorantia*, XXII, 6). But since no proof has been offered that she knew of the impediment which invalidated, and since spiritual disharmony began in a very short time and lasted till the sentence of divorce, it cannot be suggested that there was a renewal of consent on Consuela's part.

9. All these things having been considered and carefully weighed, invoking the name of Christ, we the undersigned Auditors, sitting as a court and having God alone before our eyes, confirming the sentence of the Diocese of Southwark, declare and give definitive sentence: "*Constare de matrimonii nullitate inter Consuelam Vanderbilt et Carolum De Marlborough*," and thus

to the question proposed we answer: "Affirmative", further deciding that the same Consuela Vanderbilt is to pay all the expenses of the case.

Romae, in sede Tribunalis S.R. Rotae, die 29 iulii, 1926.
      Henricus Quattrocolo, Ponens
      Franciscus Morano
      Arcturus Wynen

L.D.S.
Ex cancellaria, die 7 augusti, 1926
      T. Tani, Notarius.

FIGURES OF ROTA CASES

CASES come up to the Roman Rota from all over the world. It is not possible to say what proportion they bear to *all* the cases of nullity decided in a given period, because, as has been said, the *defensor vinculi* is not bound to appeal to the Rota: he may, at his choice, appeal instead to the court of the Metropolitan. Canonists I have consulted express the opinion that the majority of cases go to the Rota. All English cases and—I am told—all cases from the United States go there.

In preparing the second edition of this book, I obtained from the N.C.W.C. News Service figures both as to the number of cases heard recently and as to the proportion of cases where the applicants were too poor to pay their own expenses. I add this information to that which I obtained for the first edition, published in 1932.

When it is remembered that the Rota is a court of appeal and that the petitions which go there have already been held as good in a diocesan court, it is surprising that practically 50 per cent of cases fail at this second hurdle.

(i) *The Number of Cases*

In the eleven years 1920–1930, 347 petitions for nullity were dealt with. Of these

> 175 were granted
> 172 were refused.

This gives an average of just on sixteen decrees of nullity per year.

In the fifteen years 1936–1950, there were 1314 petitions. Of these

> 528 were granted
> 786 were refused.

The average is just on thirty-five decrees of nullity per year.

In 1956 there were over 382,000 divorces in the U.S.A.

Nullity, in other words, is not a way of giving divorces under another name: it is true that nullities are granted in certain cases by the Diocesan Court without any need of appeal to the Rota, and these are not counted in the figures given above. But they are open-and-shut cases— it will hardly be suggested that the Church forbids priests or people with a spouse living, for instance, to marry, or requires Catholics to be married by a priest, simply in order to leave a loophole for escape from marriage.

(ii) *Cases in Which Applicants Were Too Poor to Pay the Expenses*

The charges are small. Costs are taxed on a regular scale, and are far lower than in a civil court. In an N.C.W.C. Report (12 May 1952) a Canon Law expert

in Washington is quoted as saying that expenses of a
case in the Rota vary widely—according to the individual case and the time required for a decision—often
totalling between $100 and $500. If the parties are too
poor to pay even these expenses, then no charge at all is
made; any priest or layman admitted to practice as an
advocate in Ecclesiastical Courts is bound to take up their
case, free of charge, when ordered to do so.

I give exact figures for the four years ending 1930[1] and
for the four years 1952–4 and 1956 (I did not get 1955
figures).

IN THE FOUR YEARS ENDING 1930

Number of cases heard 207
Number in which applicants paid their
    own expenses 111
Number of these successful .... 39 (or 35%)
Number in which applicants could not
    pay 96
Number of these successful .... 40 (or 41%)

IN THE FOUR YEARS 1952–4 AND 1956

Number of cases heard 859
Number in which applicants paid their
    own expenses 497

[1] *Acta Apostolicae Sedis*, 1928, p. 43; 1929, p. 78; 1930, p. 177;
1931, p. 89.

Number of these successful 217 (44%)
Number in which applicants could not
    pay 362
Number of these successful 175 (48%)

FURTHER READING

The best reading on the Catholic Law of Nullity is to be found in

(a) The *Codex Juris Canonici*, Pars I, Lib.III, Tit.VII (Canons 1012–1143)

(b) The decisions of actual cases reported in *Acta Apostolicae Sedis*, particularly before 1921.

Books in English on the Church's Law of Marriage are *Christian Marriage* by G. H. Joyce, S.J. (Sheed & Ward), Smet's *Betrothment and Marriage* (2 vols., Herder) and *Marriage, Contract and Sacrament* by James Risk, S.J. (Callaghan and Company, Chicago).

A Practical Commentary on the Code of Canon Law by Stanislaus Woywod, O.F.M., and Callistus Smith, O.F.M., contains an excellent section on Marriage.

A remarkable work is *The Canon Law Digest* issued every few years by T. Lincoln Bouscaren, S.J., and published by the Bruce Company of Milwaukee. It contains newly issued Documents Affecting the Code of Canon Law—including Documents or Decided Cases on the Law of Nullity. There are now four volumes, the last published in 1958.

For English law, there are Latey *On Divorce*, 14th edition 1952, and Tolstoy *On Divorce*, 4th edition 1958 (both Sweet and Maxwell, London) and Rayden *On Divorce*, 7th edition 1958 (Butterworth, London).

For New York law, there is *New York Law of Domestic Relations* by M. L. Grossman (Dennis & Co., Buffalo); and Clevenger's *Annulment of Marriage* (Mathew Bender, New York).

On American marriage law generally—*Personal and Domestic Relations* by J. W. Madden (West Publishing Company, St. Paul), Nelson *On Divorce and Annulment* (3 vols., Callaghan and Company, Chicago).

Such of these books as are out of print will be found in any good law library.

Index of Cases